SHAKESPEARE
and his world

F. E. HALLIDAY

SHAKESPEARE

and his world

With 151 illustrations

CHARLES SCRIBNER'S SONS
NEW YORK

To BARBARA HEPWORTH in Friendship and Admiration

Originally published in the United States in 1956
by The Viking Press, Inc.

1 3 5 7 9 11 13 15 17 19   I/C   20 18 16 14 12 10 8 6 4 2

Printed and bound in Singapore by
FEP International Pte Ltd.
Library of Congress Catalog Card Number 79–63700

SBN 0–684–16287–3

It is, unfortunately, a common delusion that little or nothing is known about the life of Shakespeare. In fact quite a lot is known. Thanks to the devoted labours of a succession of English and American scholars, from Malone and Halliwell-Phillipps in the eighteenth and nineteenth centuries to C. W. Wallace and Leslie Hotson in our own day, much has been discovered, and still is being discovered; far more, indeed, than we had any right to expect concerning a dramatist who lived the greater part of his life, and died, in an obscure provincial town. For it must be remembered that plays were not treated as serious literature when Shakespeare was alive, that after his death his work was temporarily eclipsed by the flashy drama of Beaumont and Fletcher, and that for the twenty years of the Civil War and Commonwealth the theatres were closed. It was, therefore, more than half a century after his death before the first fumbling attempts at research began, too late to glean much first-hand biographical information. But since then much has been unearthed from record and contemporary allusion, and the object of this book is quite simply to describe what we know about Shakespeare's life after three centuries of discovery, and to illuminate and animate the story by illustration.

It is doubly unfortunate that it should so generally be assumed that we know little about Shakespeare. For one thing, it has helped to foster the sentimental eighteenth century conception of Shakespeare as an inspired peasant, a conception that there is no longer any excuse for holding, yet one which in turn has encouraged the theory that such a man could not have written the plays attributed to him. A hundred years ago a Miss Delia Bacon proved to her own satisfaction that her namesake Francis Bacon was the author. Miss Bacon died insane, but her work was carried on by her disciples until they themselves were assailed by those who professed to have found 'the real Shakespeare' in one or other of a group of noble earls. Now we are told that the real author was Marlowe. Soon somebody in search of a hobby will discover the shadowy Elizabethan dramatist Wentworth Smith, and the Smithites will join in the cry.

Although this book has not been written to refute this nonsense, it should do something incidentally to dispel it. So far as I am aware nothing quite like it has been attempted before, and the illustration of so much biographical material, documents as well as portraits and places, should serve as a reassurance that the man who wrote the thirty-six plays of the Folio was William Shakespeare of Stratford-upon-Avon. It is a reasonable hypothesis.

F.E.H.

St. Ives
Cornwall
Summer 1956

CONTENTS

Warwick, from the low hills of Budbrooke

THERE HAVE BEEN SHAKESPEARES in Warwickshire since at least the middle of the thirteenth century, at which time a William Sakspere lived at Clopton on the outskirts of Stratford. This medieval William, however, was no great credit to the family, for, more than three hundred years before the birth of his famous namesake, he was hanged for robbery. 'Sakspere' is merely a simple variant of the name, which could be spelt in a bewildering number of ways, shading gradually into forms remoter and more remote from the generally accepted 'Shakespeare': Shakespèrt, Schakosper, Shexsper, Saxpere, Sashpierre, Chacsper, Sadspere, Shaksbye, Shaxbee, and even Shakeschafte and Shakstaff. Seventeenth century antiquaries favoured a heroic derivation—'*Martial* in the *Warlike* sound of his Sur-name (whence some may conjecture him of a Military extraction), *Hasti-vibrans*, or Shake-speare'—but as only one Warwickshire family of Shakespeares is known to have held land by military tenure such a picturesque interpretation is open to doubt.

The poet's grandfather was probably the Richard Shakyspere who in 1525 was living at Budbrooke on the low hills that look eastward towards Warwick. A few years later he moved to the village of Snitterfield, three miles north of Stratford, where he farmed land on the manor of Robert Arden, the head of a

Warwickshire
in the time of
Shakespeare.
John Speed's
map, 1610

9

Snitterfield Church, where Shakespeare's father was christened

minor branch of an old and distinguished Warwickshire family. It was at Snitterfield that Richard's two sons, John and Henry, were born, probably in the fifteen-thirties, and christened in the parish church.

Robert Arden did not live at Snitterfield, but at Wilmcote, a village three or four miles to the west, where he had another estate. There, in his fine half-timbered farmhouse, backed by substantial barns and a great stone dovecote, he brought up a family of eight daughters, the youngest of whom was Mary. For almost thirty years Shakespeare's two grandfathers were neighbours, separated only by a few furlongs of road, and bound to one another by a common interest in the land, of which one was owner and the other tenant.

Robert Arden's house at Wilmcote, where Shakespeare's mother was born

Aston Cantlow Church, probably where Shakespeare's parents were married

John Shakespeare must have known Mary Arden ever since he was a small boy, and when, about 1550, he moved to Stratford, leaving his father and brother to carry on the farm at Snitterfield, he was still only a bare hour's walk from her home. No doubt the humble farmer's son felt it necessary to better his condition if ever he was to win the hand of the daughter of a country gentleman, however unpretentious, and in Stratford he set up as a glove-maker. His business prospered, and shortly after the death of Robert Arden in 1556 he married Mary, presumably in the church of Aston Cantlow, within the parish of which Wilmcote lies. It was a good match for the ambitious young man, for, apart from her name and social standing, Mary brought him two properties at Wilmcote, some hundred and fifty acres in all, and a share in the reversion of the Snitterfield estate.

But John too owned property. He was doing well, and just before his marriage invested money in two Stratford houses, one of which was in the row that ran along the north side of Henley Street at the top of the town. This was the one to the east of the 'Birthplace', in which he may already have been living as tenant. He had been in Henley Street for some time, for in 1552 he and his friend Adrian Quiney had been fined, not unreasonably, for making a dunghill in that thoroughfare. If, then, it was to the 'Birthplace' that he brought his bride, presumably he moved his business into the newly-bought house next door.

Their first child was born in September 1558. Nothing more is known of her, and it seems likely that she died in infancy, as did her sister, who was only five months old when she was buried in April, 1563. Perhaps both were victims of the plague, the fearful scourge that ravaged England with exceptional ferocity in 1563, and hope must have been seasoned with dread in the hearts of John and Mary Shakespeare as the time approached for the birth of their third child. But plague disappeared with the frosts of winter, and when pear and apple were breaking into blossom in the April of 1564 a son was born, perhaps on the 23rd. He was called William, and on the 26th 'Gulielmus filius Johannes Shakspere' was christened in the parish church of the Holy Trinity.

Queen Elizabeth was then a woman of thirty. Six years before she had succeeded to the throne of England, a backward and bankrupt island on the fringe merely of the new civilisation of the Renaissance. Thanks, however, to her remarkable courage and

Shakespeare's Birthplace

The first known view, 1769
Before restoration, 1847
During restoration, 1857
As it looks to-day

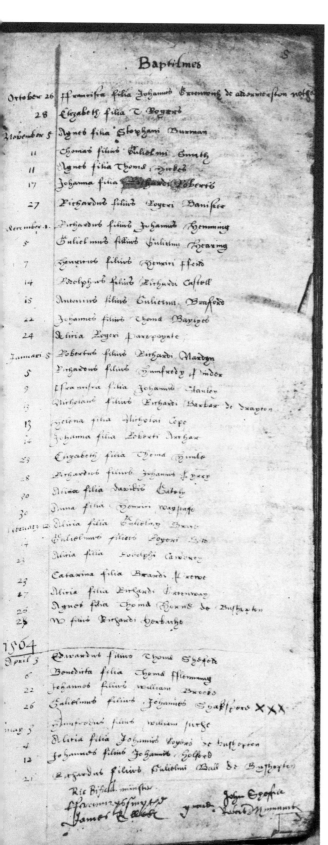

Baptismes

Queen Elizabeth I when she was thirty-five and Shakespeare five

Baptism of 'William, son of John Shakspere', 26 April 1564. The entry in Stratford Parish Register

William Cecil, Lord Burghley,
Queen Elizabeth's chief minister

ability she had already set the country on the highroad to fortune. Above all, she had united the great majority of her people by establishing a moderate form of Protestantism as the official religion, though there still remained some dis-affected Catholics, and on the other flank discontented Puritans who thought the Reformation had not gone far enough. In all her measures she had been advised and helped by her Secretary, William Cecil, Lord Burghley, who was to serve her with unwavering devotion almost to the end of her reign.

But one thing Elizabeth could not do, directly at least—summon up writers to enrich the literature of England which, since the death of Chaucer a hundred and fifty years before, had been lamentably barren. There were musicians equal to any in Europe, notably Thomas Tallis and his pupil William Byrd, but where were the poets? Indirectly, however, she might do much.

Then there was another thing that Elizabeth *would* not do—marry. She flirted and, for diplomatic ends, made a great show of marital intentions, but the most likely man seemed to be her favourite, Robert Dudley, Earl of Leicester, to whom she had just granted Kenilworth Castle. Leicester was un-popular and unacceptable—he was suspected of having murdered his first wife

Robert Dudley, Earl of Leicester,
Queen Elizabeth's first favourite

—but marry she must, for the heir to the throne was the flighty Catholic Mary, Queen of Scots, who was on the point of marrying her vicious young cousin, Lord Darnley. Cecil was in a frenzy of anxiety, yet Elizabeth remained obstinately unmarried.

Every summer Elizabeth took a holiday in the form of a progress, or state tour, when she and her Court, with immense quantities of baggage, descended upon the houses of those chief subjects who were fortunate—or unfortunate—enough to be within easy range of the capital. In August, 1566, she spent a few days with Leicester at Kenilworth, calling on his brother, the Earl of Warwick, at Warwick Castle, on her way to stay at Charlecote, the recently rebuilt house of Sir Thomas Lucy near Stratford. It was probably as she left on that August day that Shakespeare, then aged two and a half, caught his first

Charlecote, the home of Sir Thomas Lucy, where Elizabeth stayed

glimpse of the Queen as she passed under the great gateway and turned south towards Banbury and Oxford. Elizabeth would see no more of Stratford than the church on the far side of the river, gleaming in the morning sun.

Stratford

The Church of the Holy Trinity stands at the south end of the town, its lofty chancel and tower (the spire was added after Shakespeare's day) mirrored in the waters of the Avon. For over two centuries it had been a collegiate church, served by priests who lived in the neighbouring College, but twenty years before Shakespeare's time the College had been dissolved, and the house occupied by the Combe family. From church and College the road bends left until it joins the broad street that intersects the little town from south to north. The houses are of brick and timber, for the nearest stone is that of the Cotswolds some miles away, and here at the very heart are the Gild buildings: the alms-houses, the Gildhall with the long schoolroom of the Grammar School above it, and the lovely spectral-grey Gild Chapel. The religious and social Gild of the Holy Cross had once been a power in the town, but like the College it had been suppressed, and the government was now in the hands of a bailiff, aldermen and capital burgesses. On the corner facing the Gild Chapel was New Place, a large half-timbered house built by Sir Hugh Clopton shortly

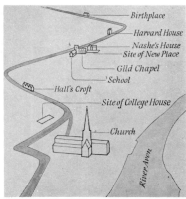

Stratford-upon-Avon. The road, imperishably associated
with Shakespeare, from his birthplace to the church

Holy Trinity Church, Stratford, where Shakespeare was baptised and buried ▶

The Gildhall with Schoolroom above

before he was buried in the church in 1492. Sir Hugh's also is the many-arched medieval bridge at the north end, the only link with London and the east, for the town was built entirely on the western bank of the river. When Shakespeare was a child it was a typical market town of some two thousand inhabitants, most of them engaged in agriculture or small-scale industry such as his father's trade of glove-making. No doubt the streets were filthy, but they were broad, and most of the houses had gardens. Then, from Henley Street the boy could roam through the remains of the Forest of Arden in the direction of Henley, Warwick, Alcester and Bidford, or he could cross the bridge and within an hour be at the foot of the Cotswolds, shapely uplands studded with beeches and grey limestone villages. And there was always the river for his delight.

The Gild Chapel, as Shakespeare saw it from New Place ▶

Clopton Bridge over the River Avon, Stratford's link with London

Education

In 1561 Richard Shakespeare had died at Snitterfield, where his younger son Henry now managed the farm. Henry was a shiftless character, always in difficulties, but his brother John pursued his prosperous career in Stratford. In 1565 he became an alderman, and by 1571, having held the coveted office of bailiff, was a sort of elder statesman, chief alderman of the borough and a justice of the peace. There were now three more children, Gilbert, Joan and Anne. William, aged seven, was old enough to go to school.

It is high time that the mischievous conception of Shakespeare as an inspired peasant was finally dispelled. His mother was a member of a great family, his father an ambitious and exceptionally able man of business, and though there is no record (why should there be?) of his schooling, it is inconceivable that such parents would let slip the opportunity of sending him to the local grammar school. For the sons of burgesses the education was free up to the age of sixteen,

The Cotswolds near Stratford, much frequented by Shakespeare and the characters in his plays

The schoolroom where Shakespeare learned his Latin

and moreover it was one of the best schools in the country. We must, therefore, imagine Shakespeare during the decade of the seventies sitting at his desk in the schoolroom over the Council Chamber, where his father helped to shape the fortunes of the town, first at the feet of Simon Hunt, a devout Catholic at heart, and then of the Welshman, Thomas Jenkins, whom he was later lovingly to caricature as Sir Hugh Evans in *The Merry Wives*. The course would be a liberal one, chiefly in Latin, and with the aid of Lily's Latin Grammar he would work his way through the easy classics, fall in love with Ovid, read some Virgil, and perhaps some of the comedies of Plautus and tragedies of Seneca. His Bible was probably the popular Genevan version of 1560, rather than the official Bishops' Bible of 1568.

His schooldays were stirring times for England. Mary, Queen of Scots, having

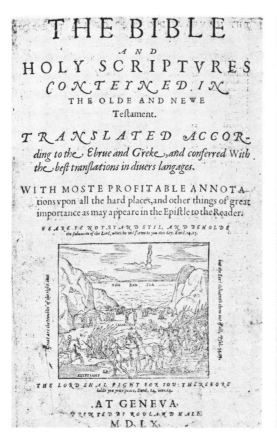

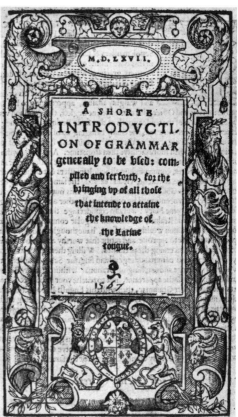

The Genevan, or 'Breeches', Bible   Lily's Latin Grammar, as used by Shakespeare

murdered her husband, had sought refuge in England where she was kept in close custody, and her son James VI, a sickly boy of Shakespeare's age, reigned in her stead. Then, the Counter-Reformation had been launched by the Pope. Philip II of Spain had driven his Protestant subjects in the Netherlands into revolt; France was in the throes of a religious war (it was while Elizabeth was staying at Charlecote on St. Bartholomew's day, 1572, that the Catholics had massacred the Huguenots in Paris); Elizabeth herself had been excommunicated, and there had been a Catholic rising and plots against her life. She still managed to keep England out of open war with Spain, but Drake was raiding the West Indies and Spanish Main, and in 1577 had set off on the voyage that was to take him round the world.

The seventies were also stirring times in the little world of the theatre. The

Sir Francis Drake after his voyage round the world, 1577-80

medieval miracle plays were still occasionally performed in the traditional manner, as at Coventry, only twenty miles from Stratford, where a series of biblical scenes was enacted by the gildsmen on movable stages, or 'pageants'. Smaller places had to be content with more modest productions within the arena formed by a circular bank of earth or by tiers of wooden steps erected to accommodate the audience. Around the arena were ranged a number of canvas 'houses', rather like bathing-tents, representing the scenes in the play. The mouth of hell was on the north side, and at the east was Heaven, a wooden hut with the throne of God, approached by steps from a projecting stage. The actors waited in their houses until called upon to perform, when they stepped into the arena to play their parts, for it was here that almost all the action took place, the stage being reserved for very exalted action in which God appeared.

But by the beginning of Elizabeth's reign the religious drama was already a curiosity, a relic of another age. In schools and at the university boys and young men were producing Latin plays in their dining-halls, and troupes of actors were wandering about the country performing 'interludes', knockabout farcical entertainments that were half acrobatic displays. The obvious place for their performance was in the medieval 'rounds', where they survived, or in the yard of an inn with its surrounding galleries. There were, however, more serious interludes, though scarcely plays in our sense of the word, written for private performance in the houses of the nobility and at Court. Small companies of players were retained to perform them, mainly in the Christmas season, after which they were free to pick up a living as best they could in London or the provinces. When Shakespeare was a boy, then, the drama was in a sorry state. The Reformation had almost killed the religious drama, and as yet the Renaissance had produced no comparable secular drama to take its place. Actors were treated as rogues and vagabonds, as many of them were, and there were no public theatres.

Miracle plays were still performed when Shakespeare was a boy

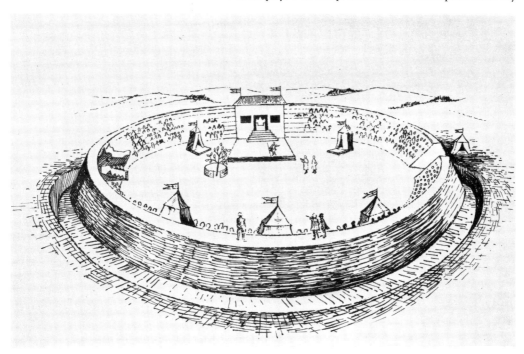

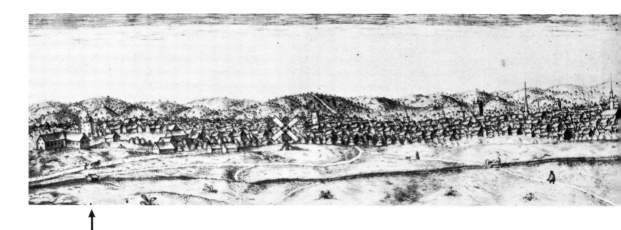

Shortly before Shakespeare's birth, however, there had been a development of great significance. Nicholas Udall, headmaster of Eton, had written a comedy modelled on Plautus for performance by boys, and Thomas Sackville and Thomas Norton a tragedy in the manner of Seneca, for presentation at Court by the students of the Inner Temple. The one, *Ralph Roister Doister,* is the first regular comedy in English, the other, *Gorboduc,* the first regular tragedy. Moreover *Gorboduc* was the first play to be written in blank verse. Here then were two plays whose classical dramatic structure might serve as a model to the shapeless episodic native interludes.

Then in the seventies came two more important developments. Acting was officially recognised as a legitimate profession, provided the player was under the patronage of a peer of the realm, and in 1576 the first public playhouse was built in London. The enterprise and vision were those of James Burbage, an obstinate ex-joiner and actor in the Earl of Leicester's company. Wisely he built The Theatre, as he proudly called it, in the rapidly expanding suburb of Shoreditch to the north of the City walls, beyond the control of the puritanical Corporation for whom the makeshift theatres in the City inns were 'meere brothel houses of Bauderie'. As we should expect, the Theatre was a combination of medieval round and inn-yard, a wooden amphitheatre of two or three galleries surrounding an open arena with projecting stage, in which the players could tumble about to their hearts' content.

Burbage soon had a competitor, for within a year the Curtain sprang up a few hundred yards nearer the City, cunningly placed to skim off a potential Theatre audience. There was also competition of another kind. The fastidious Elizabeth naturally preferred the more civilised and musical performances given by boys to the boisterous efforts of the uncouth adult actors, so that, encouraged by her favour, the Master of her choirboys rented a large room in the dissolved Blackfriars priory by the river, where they gave public performances of their

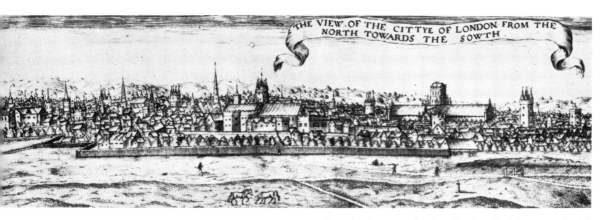

London in 1600, showing the Curtain Theatre on the left

Title page of the first blank verse play

The Curtain Theatre,
where Shakespeare and his company
played from 1597 to 1599.
A detail from the view above

plays before production at Court. The choirboys of St. Paul's also had their
little playhouse, so that by 1577 there were two open public theatres, and two
roofed, or private, theatres. But again, where were the poets and dramatists to
write for them?

Shakespeare, of course, knew nothing of these developments, though they
had their effect even in Stratford. As early as 1569, when his father was bailiff,
the Queen's Interluders, banished from Court for their incompetence, had
visited the town, when they gave a first performance in the Council Chamber
before being licensed to play elsewhere to the public. Then, in the seventies
Stratford had become a regular centre for touring companies, notably the Earl
of Leicester's, and naturally it was the Earl's company who helped to entertain
the Queen when she stayed at Kenilworth in the summer of 1575. The
'Pleasures' were on a princely scale, and no doubt Shakespeare played truant on
the day of the great water-pageant of the Lady of the Lake, and wondered at
Arion riding on a dolphin's back.

In this year his father bought more Stratford property, but soon afterwards
his fortunes began to decline. If he was a Catholic, as is possible, he may have

The site of the boys' theatre at Blackfriars

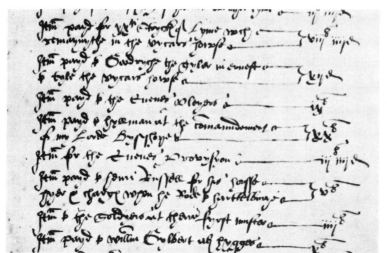

'Item payd to the Quenes Players iv^x',
by the Stratford Council,
when Shakespeare's father was bailiff, 1568-9

The entertainment of Queen Elizabeth referred to by Shakespeare in *A Midsummer Night's Dream*

been crippled by fines imposed under the increasingly severe recusancy measures, or he may have got involved in the affairs of his brother Henry, as he certainly did later, but whatever the cause, by 1579 he was reduced to mortgaging his wife's Wilmcote property and selling her share in the Snitterfield estate. The eight-year-old Anne died in the same year, but a third son, Richard, had been born in 1574, and to add to his troubles another child was expected soon. However, William would be sixteen in the following April, when he would leave school and be able to help in the business. This, then, was the position in the Henley Street house in the spring of 1580, as Drake approached Plymouth after his voyage round the world; John Shakespeare was in difficulties, and had five children to support: the baby Edmund, Richard aged six, Joan eleven, Gilbert fourteen, and William just sixteen. But William was now an asset rather than a liability, though one suspects that he was less interested in his father's business than in the three exciting books that had just been published: John Lyly's romance, *Euphues*, Thomas North's translation of Plutarch, and Edmund Spenser's *Shepherd's Calendar*, dedicated to Philip Sidney. The literary renaissance had begun.

In later life Shakespeare was to prove an admirable man of affairs, but as a boy he must have found the routine of business a deadly frustration, when he longed for leisure to read, and above all to write. Yet he would find some time for his adolescent scribbling, no doubt songs, sonnets and blank verse in the manner of Wyatt and Surrey, whose poems had been published shortly before his birth, and pastorals like those of the new man, Spenser. And in the course of the next two years, the hazel-eyed and auburn-haired boy—if we may trust

The *Golden Hind*, the ship in which Drake sailed round the world

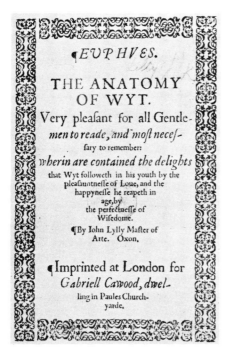

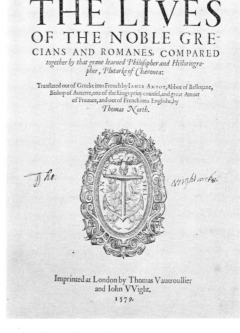

A book that influenced Shakespeare   The book used by Shakespeare for his Roman plays

the colouring on his monument—grew into a 'handsome, well-shaped' young man, just such a young man to entangle the heart of a woman.

Across the meadows on the western fringe of Stratford lay the village of Shottery, and the thatched half-timbered farmhouse where Richard Hathaway lived with his second wife and numerous children. Richard died in 1581, and the next we hear of the family is of the proposed marriage of his eldest child, Anne, to 'William Shagspere'. Perhaps the ardent and frustrated boy of eighteen was infatuated by the woman eight years his senior, but Anne, whose chances of marriage were rapidly receding, did nothing to discourage him. By November 1582 it was impossible to conceal the fact that she was with child, and Shakespeare had to apply to the Bishop of Worcester for a special licence that would allow them to be married with only once asking of the banns. The clerk who recorded the issue of the licence muddled his entry and wrote that it was for 'Willelmum Shaxpere and Annam Whateley de Temple Grafton'. It was a very human error, for on the same day there had been a suit involving a certain William Whateley; and that it was an error is clear from the bond into which two Shottery farmers entered on the following day, November 28th, exempting

Marriage

Temple Grafton Church, probably where Shakespeare and Anne Hathaway were married

Fulk Sandells and John Richardson guarantee the validity
of the proposed marriage of 'William Shagspere and Anne Hathwey'

The Hathaway farmhouse at Shottery

The clerk records the issue of a marriage licence
for 'William Shaxpere and Anne Whateley of Temple Grafton'

the bishop from liability if any irregularity should turn up after the hasty marriage. There was nothing unusual in the proceeding, and as Shakespeare was a minor he had to have such sureties. The couple would be married within a few days, probably at the village mentioned by the clerk, Temple Grafton, beyond Shottery, to escape over-curious eyes.

In accordance with the custom of the day Anne would join the family of John and Mary Shakespeare in Henley Street, where her first child, Susanna, was born in May, 1583. Her husband now seemed doomed to spend his days as a small trader in Stratford. It is true that his brother Gilbert was old enough to take his place in the family business, but William had trapped himself, or been trapped, by his marriage, and when in February, 1585 'Hamnet and Judeth sonne and daughter to William Shakspere' were christened there seemed to be no escape. Yet escape he did.

A late tradition has it that he was forced to 'fly his native country' by Sir Thomas Lucy of Charlecote, for poaching deer in his park, a picturesque though unlikely story based perhaps upon some petty trespass. According to another tradition he was for a time 'a schoolmaster in the country', some say at Dursley in the south Cotswolds, others at Rufford in Lancashire. Then there are those who think he went off to the Netherlands with the expeditionary force under Leicester, after the outbreak of open war with Spain in 1585, or,

The baptism of Shakespeare's children:
Susanna, 26 May 1583
The twins, Hamnet and Judith, 2 Feb. 1585

Hampton Lucy from Charlecote Park, scene of the poaching legend

most unlikely of all, to Italy. The chances are that he went to London when he could no longer bear the humdrum life to which he was condemned. Every year Stratford was visited by two or three companies of players, one of them Worcester's with their recent find, Edward Alleyn, two years younger than Shakespeare; and when five companies came in 1587 the attraction of London may well have proved irresistible. This was the year in which his Stratford contemporary, Richard Field, long apprenticed to a London printer, married his master's widow and took over the business. Perhaps Field had found an opening for him. In any event, Shakespeare probably went up to London in 1587, leaving his wife and three children in the care of his parents. His father seems to have been in a poor way at the time, for he had just been expelled from the borough Council, which he had not attended for many years, and

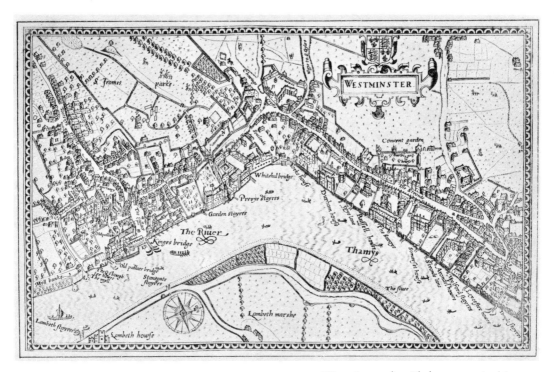

Westminster when Shakespeare arrived in 1587

sued for a debt of his brother Henry, which he had guaranteed. However, Gilbert was now twenty-one, and Joan, aged eighteen, would be a great help in the home. William was twenty-three.

London

There were two possible routes to London. After crossing Clopton bridge he could either fork right in the direction of Oxford, or he could go straight on through Banbury and Grendon, where he is said to have found the constable who was the original of Dogberry. The roads converged shortly before reaching Westminster, the seat of the central government where the great nobles had their town houses. As he walked wondering towards the City, he would pass between the old Palace of Westminster and the Abbey, and under the two gateways that connected Whitehall Palace, the Queen's principal residence, with its extension on the other side of the road. At Charing Cross he would turn east along the Strand, with Convent Garden and almost open country on the one hand, and on the other the great houses bordering the river, York House, Durham House, Somerset House, Leicester House, which must have set him thinking of Kenilworth. Then came the Inns of Court, like university colleges, where the lawyers learned their profession and the gentry how to manage their estates, and at Ludgate he entered the City.

Whitehall Palace and the great houses bordering the river

Westminster was splendid and spacious, though he had seen something like it before, at Oxford. But he had never seen anything like the City into which he now plunged, a city of 150,000 inhabitants, most of them huddled within the walls, though the suburbs to the north were rapidly growing. The brick and timber gabled houses of the merchants and shopkeepers were familiar enough, but it was the size of the place that was so unexpected and over-whelming, a town as big, or at least as populous, as a hundred Stratfords. The main thoroughfare led up Ludgate Hill, dominated by the decaying fabric of medieval St. Paul's, whose spire had fallen some years ago, and where Sir Philip Sidney had recently been buried. Then along Cheapside and Cornhill into Gracious Street, cutting through the City from south to north, the street of the great inns such as the Boar's Head, in whose yards plays were still per-formed. If he turned north he would soon find himself at Bishopsgate and on the road to the suburban Curtain and Theatre, if south he would come to the river and London Bridge. This was the only bridge across the Thames, many arched and lined with tall houses forming another street. Below was the Tower and the port of London, for only the smaller craft could sail beneath the arches. At the southern end, aloft on poles, were the heads of the traitors who had been

I V I T A S

This description of
Famous Citty LONDON Wa_
The feare of Christe 1600
feare of the Moste Wished
Raigne of the Right Reno_
ELISABETH The Fort_
Sr Nicholas Moseley Knigh_
Maior And Roger Clarke_
Wylde Sherifes of The

By the industrie of
Ihon Norden
...

Shakespeare's London

Mary, Queen of Scots, executed shortly before Shakespeare's arrival in London

executed after the discovery of the latest Catholic plot.

Shakespeare had arrived in London at one of the most exciting moments in its history. The plot had been to murder Elizabeth, rescue Mary, Queen of Scots, and with the help of Spain put her on the throne. Reluctantly Elizabeth had agreed that her cousin Mary was too dangerous to live longer, and in February she had been executed. The crisis of the war was at hand, for, in spite of Drake's dazzling raid on Cadiz, Philip II of Spain was building an Armada that would sail in the following year if not in this, and London was urgently preparing to meet invasion.

The year 1587 was also to prove one of the most exciting in the history of the theatre. If Shakespeare had crossed the river into Southwark, passed the church of St. Mary Overy, he would have come to Bankside, a region of prisons and brothels, where he would see—and smell—the Beargarden, and a similar cylindrical building just nearing completion, the Rose theatre. This was the work of Philip Henslowe, an enterprising and not over-scrupulous pawn-broker who foresaw a profitable future for the theatrical business. He had good reasons. There were now a number of reputable companies of players whose standard of acting was rapidly improving, and quite recently the Queen herself had taken a company of twelve of the leading players under her patronage. But more important, there had appeared a group of young university men who were writing plays that really were plays, and not mere knockabout entertainments.

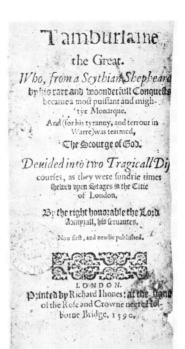

The first of Lyly's plays
to be performed at Court

Marlowe's *Tamburlaine*, one of
the first plays seen by
Shakespeare in London

There was John Lyly of Oxford, who had written a number of light sophis-
ticated comedies for the children's company at Blackfriars. It is true that their
little private theatre had recently been closed—so much the better for the Rose—
but Lyly was popular with the Queen and still writing for the Children of
Paul's who played at their singing-school near the cathedral, as well as at Court.
Then there was another, though less respectable Oxford man, George Peele, and
the brilliant and improvident Robert Greene of Cambridge. Perhaps Henslowe
had also met Peele's Oxford contemporary, Thomas Lodge, and Greene's young
friend Christopher Marlowe, just come down from Cambridge with the
manuscript of a play in his pocket. And it may have been at the newly opened
Rose a few months later that Shakespeare saw Edward Alleyn, now the leading
actor of the Admiral's company, play Tamburlaine. If so, it was a revelation,
and decisive in his choice of a career. It was also a revolution, for on that afternoon, as Alleyn declaimed the poetry of Marlowe, the modern English drama
was born.

Whatever the motives that brought Shakespeare to London, he now realised
that his true vocation was to write for the theatre, a course which meant that
the poetry he ached to write could become the very stuff of his profession. But
the plays had yet to be written, and in the meantime he had to earn a living.
The obvious course was to join a company of actors, for in that way he would
learn his craft from the inside and have a likely market for his wares.

The defeat of the Spanish Armada, July 1588 ▶

A company of actors consisted of about eight men, all of whom invested capital in a common stock of plays and apparel, sharing the profits in proportion to their investments, whence the name of 'sharers', or more picturesquely, 'full adventurers'. They had two or three boy apprentices whom they trained to play women's parts, for there were no actresses on the public stage for almost another century, and they hired a few novices, or old hands with no capital to invest, to play minor parts. It would be as a 'hireling' that Shakespeare found employment, probably with the Queen's, the company for which Robert Greene was just beginning to write.

For some years, as we should expect, we hear nothing of the obscure actor and aspiring dramatist, and we must imagine him 'dressing' and rewriting old plays for his company, and trying his hand at original work, when he was not engaged in acting or rehearsing the numerous parts that he had to learn, for there was a different play each afternoon of the week, with a new one introduced into their repertory every fortnight or so. In the spring they performed in one of the public theatres, generally the Theatre, in the summer they went on tour, in 1589 getting as far afield as Carlisle, then back to their London theatre for an autumn season before retreating to one of the inns in Gracious Street for the winter, where they rehearsed the plays they were to present at Court.

The life of an actor with such a company, and at this time the Queen's was the most favoured of all, was a liberal education. Apart from the travel, the actors inevitably met the poets who wrote their plays, and mixed with the nobles and gallants of the Inns of Court who frequented their theatre, and sometimes invited them to perform in their dininghalls. Then at Christmas they performed before the Queen herself. Under Elizabeth the Court Revels began on December 26th and reached their climax on Twelfth Night, January 6th, within which Twelve Days of Christmas four or five plays were given, followed by two or three more before the beginning of Lent. Between 1587 and 1592 the Queen's Men gave fourteen of these Court performances, far more than any other company. However unpolished Shakespeare may have been when he arrived in London, it would not be long before he was at ease in the intellectual and courtly life of the capital, and he would have no difficulty in representing such a society in his plays.

Meanwhile, a new era had begun. The Armada had been destroyed, and the Spanish grip on the New World loosened. Leicester was dead, and his stepson, the handsome young Earl of Essex, had taken his place beside the aging Queen, quite eclipsing her other favourite, Sir Walter Raleigh. And, as if in celebration of these changes, the literature of England suddenly blossomed as never before. Sidney's *Arcadia* and his sonnets, and the first three books of Spenser's *Faerie Queene* were published, while in the theatre a dramatic revolution was carried

Queen Elizabeth after the destruction of the Armada

The Earl of Essex, the Queen's new favourite,
and Sir Walter Raleigh, Captain of the Guard

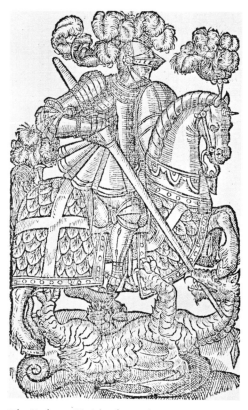

Sir Philip Sidney, killed in 1586, whose sonnets inspired Shakespeare

The Redcross Knight, from *The Faerie Queene*, published when Shakespeare was writing his first plays

through by Marlowe and the rest of the University Wits, now joined by Tom Nashe. Then there was Thomas Kyd's *Spanish Tragedy*, a play of ghosts, revenge and blood, that was to prove as perennially popular as Marlowe's *Tamburlaine*, *Faustus* and *Jew of Malta*.

Early Plays and Poems

Greene however had reached the end of his meteoric career. In September, 1592, consumed by his excesses, he lay dying in the house of a poor cobbler, where he wrote his *Groatsworth of Wit*, an autobiographical fragment addressed to his fellow dramatists, Marlowe, Nashe and Peele, imploring them to take example from his fate and not to waste their wits in writing plays, from which the only ones to profit were the players—puppets, antics, apes. But this was not all. There was a young actor, no graduate and no gentleman, but a conceited 'Shakescene', who had had the audacity to set up as dramatist and write plays that the public preferred to his. The reference is unmistakably to Shakespeare, for 'Tygers hart wrapt in a Players hyde' is a parody of a line in *Henry VI,*

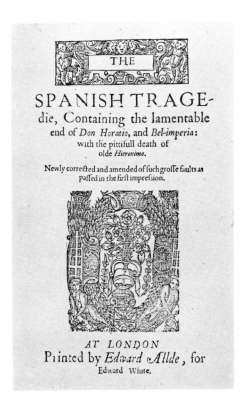

THE

SPANISH TRAGE-

die, Containing the lamentable
end of *Don Horatio*, and *Bel-imperia*:
with the pittifull death of
olde *Hieronimo*.

Newly corrected and amended of such grosse faults as
passed in the first impression.

AT LONDON
Printed by *Edward Allde*, for
Edward White.

Greenes

Sweet boy, might I aduise thee, be aduisde, and get not
many enemies by bitter wordes : inueigh against vaine
men, for thou canst do it, no man better, no man so well :
thou hast a libertie to reprooue all, and name none; for
one being spoken to, all are offended; none being blamed
no man is iniured. Stop shallow water still running, it
will rage, or tread on a worme and it will turne : then
blame not Schollers vexed with sharpe lines, if they reprooue thy too much liberty of reproofe.

And thou no lesse deseruing than the other two, in
some things rarer, in nothing inferiour ; driuen (as my
selfe) to extreme shifts, a litle haue I to say to thee: and
were it not an idolatrous oth, I would sweare by sweet
S. George, thou art vnworthy better hap, sith thou de-
pendest on so meane a stay . Base minded men all three
of you, if by my miserie you be not warnd: for vnto none
of you (like mee) sought those burres to cleaue : those
Puppets (I meane) that spake from our mouths, those
Anticks garnisht in our colours. Is it not strange, that
I, to whom they all haue beene beholding: is it not like
that you, to whome they all haue beene beholding, shall
(were yee in that case as I am now) bee both at once of
them forsaken ? Yes trust them not : for there is an vp-
start Crow, beautified with our feathers, that with his
Tygers hart wrapt in a Players hyde, supposes he is as
well able to bombast out a blanke verse as the best of
you : and beeing an absolute Iohannes fac totum, is in
his owne conceit the onely Shake-scene in a countrey.
O that I might intreat your rare wits to be imployed in
more profitable courses : & let those Apes imitate your
past excellence, and neuer more acquaint them with
your admired inuentions . I knowe the best husband of
you

Thomas Kyd's 'tragedy of revenge'   Robert Greene's attack on 'Shakescene'

Part Three. The Duke of York is addressing his captor, Queen Margaret:

> *O tiger's heart wrapped in a woman's hide!*
> *How couldst thou drain the life-blood of the child,*
> *To bid the father wipe his eyes withal,*
> *And yet be seen to bear a woman's face?*
> *Women are soft, mild, pitiful and flexible;*
> *Thou stern, obdurate, flinty, rough, remorseless.*
> *Bid'st thou me rage? why, now thou hast thy wish:*
> *Wouldst have me weep? why, now thou hast thy will:*
> *For raging wind blows up incessant showers,*
> *And when the rage allays, the rain begins.*

The verse, inflated, rhetorical and sententious, is a good example of Shakespeare's early style, modelled, as was only to be expected, on that of Marlowe.

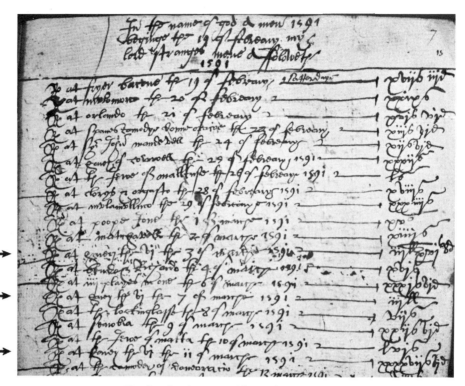

Henslowe's Diary, 1591(2): 'At harey the vj, £3.16.8'. The first record of a performance of a Shakespeare play, *Henry VI*, Part 1

Pierce Penilesse, 1592. Thomas Nashe's reference to the performance of *Henry VI*, Part 1

By the end of 1592, then, Shakespeare had written the three parts of *Henry VI* and made a considerable reputation as a dramatist. That he was a popular one is clear from the entry that Henslowe made in his accounts when Lord Strange's company played 'Harey the vj' (*Henry VI*, Part 1) at the Rose in the previous March. His takings were £3.16.8 (£100 of our money), the highest of the season, and its popularity is reflected in a passage of Nashe's *Pierce Penilesse*, describing the effect of the Talbot scenes in the play. Evidently Strange's had been buying up some of the stock of the Queen's, for they gave three of Greene's plays as well, all of them dismal failures financially.

Not unnaturally Shakespeare was offended by Greene's attack, and protested to the editor of the *Groatsworth of Wit*, Henry Chettle, who made a point of meeting him, and then in the Preface to his *Kind-Harts Dreame* handsomely apologised for leaving in the passage. It is the first description we have of Shakespeare, then aged twenty-eight, and it could scarcely be a more attractive one: civil in his demeanour, upright, well thought of by those in authority, an excellent actor and a graceful writer.

The worst enemies of the players were Puritans and plague. The Puritans, strongly entrenched in the City Corporation, would have liked to see the theatres plucked down and the prosperous and swaggering actors whipped and put to profitable employment, but since the Queen's open patronage of players they had been on the defensive. The most that Elizabeth and her Privy Council would allow was the closing of the theatres in time of plague, from which for

The first description of Shakespeare: Henry Chettle's apology in *Kind-Harts Dreame*, 1592

To the Gentlemen Readers.

fory, as if the originall fault had beene my fault, becaufe my felfe haue feene his demeanor no leffe ciuill than he exclent in the qualitie he profeffes: Befides, diuers of worfhip haue reported, his vp- rightnes of dealing, which argues his honefty, and his facetious grace in writting, that aprooues his Art. For the firft, whofe learning I reuerence, and at the perufing of Greenes Booke, ftroke out what then in confcience I thought he in fome dif- pleafure writ : or had it beene true, yet to publifh

the last ten years London had been virtually free; indeed there had been no serious outbreak since the year before Shakespeare's birth. But in the summer of 1592 the dreaded pestilence struck again, at the height of its fury claiming a thousand victims in a single week. The theatres were closed, and the companies driven unprofitably into the provinces to 'stalk upon boards and barrel-heads to an old cracked trumpet'. Winter brought no relief, 1593 was even worse, and it was the summer of 1594 before the theatres reopened.

What was Shakespeare doing during these two years? By this time we should expect him to be a sharer and no longer a hireling, but there is no record of his touring with any of the companies. A mere actor had no alternative to this unrewarding vagabondage, but Shakespeare was now primarily a writer and would be far more profitably employed in practising his craft. In Stratford he had a wife and three young children of whom he could have seen little for the last five years, and we may, I think, be pretty sure that it was with them that he spent the greater part of the period of plague. The Queen's made for Stratford soon after it began, and possibly he accompanied and left them there, arranging to rejoin them when the theatres reopened.

He would find his father still in trouble, having recently been included in a list of recusants for 'not comminge monethlie to the churche, it is sayd for feare of process for debtte'. This, however, is the last we hear of his misfortunes, probably because his successful son was able to help him put his affairs in order. They were busy years for the young dramatist. He had already written *Richard III*—creating incidentally his first great character—so rounding off the *Henry VI* trilogy, and now in his new-found happiness he turned naturally to comedy and lyric poetry. *The Comedy of Errors, The Taming of the Shrew* and *The Two Gentlemen of Verona* belong to this idyllic period, as do the early sonnets and the two long poems, *Venus and Adonis* and *The Rape of Lucrece*. Like Marlowe, he was still mainly interested in the poetry and the event, in telling a tragic, horrible, farcical or amorous story. His attitude to his characters, the serious ones at least, is detached, and there is something just a little callous in the way he moves his puppets and makes them speak and suffer. He was, in short, a healthy, happy and successful young poet of thirty. But the influence of Marlowe became progressively less, and the almost brutal martial music of his master's characteristic line was transformed into a more flexible and dancing measure, even in *Richard III*:

> *And now, instead of mounting barbed steeds*
> *To fright the souls of fearful adversaries,*
> *He capers nimbly in a lady's chamber*
> *To the lascivious pleasing of a lute.*

VENVS
AND ADONIS

Vilia miretur vulgus : mihi flauus Apollo
Pocula Castalia plena ministret aqua.

LONDON
Imprinted by Richard Field, and are to be sold at
the signe of the white Greyhound in
Paules Church-yard.
1593.

The first work of Shakespeare
to be published

Venus and Adonis, the first of his works to be published, was beautifully printed by his friend Richard Field in 1593, and proved so popular that it went through nine editions in as many years. Every author tried to find a patron, and so he dedicated his poem hopefully to Henry Wriothesley, Earl of Southampton, a wealthy and influential young man of twenty, promising him a 'graver labour' if this amorous tale met with his approval. It did, and in the following year Field printed *The Rape of Lucrece* with another dedication to Southampton.

It was the publication of Sidney's sonnets that inspired Shakespeare to try his hand at the new form, and, as in Sidney's, a story runs obscurely through the sequence. They are addressed mainly to a beautiful young man who steals

TO THE RIGHT
HONOVRABLE, HENRY
VVriothefley, Earle of Southhampton,
and Baron of Titchfield.

H E loue I dedicate to your
Lordfhip is without end:wher-
of this Pamphlet without beginning is but a fuperfluous
Moity. The warrant I haue of
your Honourable difpofition,
not the worth of my vntutord
Lines makes it affured of acceptance. VVhat I haue
done is yours, what I haue to doe is yours, being
part in all I haue, deuoted yours. VVere my worth
greater, my duety would fhew greater, meane time,
as it is, it is bound to your Lordfhip; To whom I wifh
long life ftill lengthned with all happineffe.

Your Lordfhips in all duety.

William Shakefpeare.

A 2

Dedication of *The Rape of Lucrece*

One of the two main claimants to be 'Mr. W.H.'
Henry Wriothesley, Earl of Southampton

away his mistress, a dark married woman, and then transfers his favour to another poet. Probably the story is almost as mythical as that of Venus and Adonis, and little more than a framework to support the poet's meditations on love and friendship. But when the sonnets were printed fifteen years later the publisher added an enigmatic dedication to 'Mr. W.H.', and who this W.H.— and the dark lady and rival poet—could have been has led to much throwing about of brains. There is no real clue to the lady and the poet—Chapman is the best guess—but it is of course tempting to believe that W.H. are the reversed initials of Henry Wriothesley, and that he, Shakespeare's patron, was the 'begetter' or inspirer of the sonnets. Some claim a more youthful peer, William Herbert, future Earl of Pembroke, who was only twelve in 1592. It is just possible, for Shakespeare probably knew Pembroke's mother, Sidney's sister,

Dedication of Shakespeare's
Sonnets to 'Mr.W.H.', by the
publisher, Thomas Thorpe

Another 'W.H.'
William Herbert,
Earl of Pembroke

In praise of Willobie *his* Auisa, *Hex-*ameton to the Author.

IN Lauine Land though Liuie boſt,
  There hath beene ſeene a Conſtant *dame:*
  Though Rome *lament that ſhe haue loſt*
  The Gareland *of her rareſt fame,*
    Yet now we ſee, that here is found,
    As great a Faith *in* Engliſh *ground.*

Though Collatine *haue deerely bought,*
To high renowne, a laſting life,
And found, that moſt in vaine haue ſought,
To haue a Faire, *and* Conſtant *wife,*
  Yet Tarquyne *pluckt his gliſtering grape,*
  And Shake-ſpeare, *paints poore* Lucrece *rape.*

Willobie his Avisa, 1594. The first literary reference to Shakespeare by name

CANT. XLIIII.

Henrico Willobego. Italo-Hiſpalenſis.

H. W. being ſodenly infected with the contagion of a fantaſticall fit, at the firſt ſight of *A*, pyneth a while in ſecret griefe, at length not able any longer to indure the burning heate of ſo feruent a humour, bewrayeth the ſecreſy of his diſeaſe vnto his familiar frend W. S. who not long before had tryed the cur-
teſy

Was Henry Willoughby 'Mr. W.H.'?

and visited their house at Wilton, frequented by so many poets of the period. There is another possibility. In 1594 Henry Willoughby, an Oxford undergraduate, published *Willobie his Avisa,* a poem lamenting his unrequited love for the virtuous Avisa. In the prose introduction to one of the cantos H.W. tells how he confided his grief to his 'familiar friend W.S.', an 'old player' at the game of love, who had just recovered from a like passion. Perhaps H.W. is Mr. W.H., and that the reference is to Shakespeare and his affair with the dark lady is made slightly more probable by the mention of *The Rape of Lucrece* in the commendatory verses prefixed to the poem. At least the line has the merit of being the first literary reference to Shakespeare by name. But the hypothesis is not very convincing, and if W.H. really was Shakespeare's friend he may have been any one of a hundred young men of whom we have never heard. More prosaically, he may merely have been the man who secured a manuscript copy of the sonnets for Thomas Thorpe to publish without Shakespeare's permission.

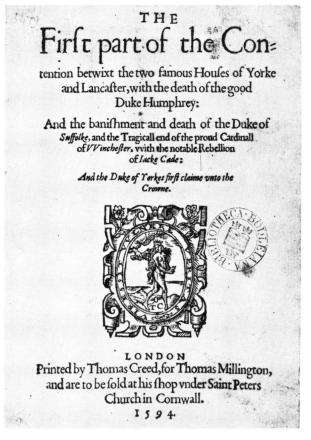

THE
First part of the Contention betwixt the two famous Houses of Yorke and Lancaster, with the death of the good Duke Humphrey:

And the banifhment and death of the Duke of Suffolke, and the Tragicall end of the proud Cardinall of VVinchefter, vvith the notable Rebellion of Iacke Cade:

And the Duke of Yorkes firft claime vnto the Crowne.

LONDON
Printed by Thomas Creed, for Thomas Millington, and are to be fold at his fhop vnder Saint Peters Church in Cornwall.
1594.

The 'Bad' Quarto of *Henry VI,* Part 2, 1594, one of the first of Shakespeare's plays to be published

Such literary piracy was only too common in Shakespeare's day, when there was no copyright in our sense of the word. All books, plays and pamphlets were supposed to be entered in the Register of the Stationers' Company, who protected the publisher, on payment of his sixpence, from any infringement of his rights, but there was nobody to protect the luckless author or the company of actors to whom he had sold a play—normally for £5 or £6—from an unscrupulous publisher who managed to get hold of a copy. The companies therefore took great care of their manuscript plays, rarely making more than one copy, but sometimes an actor memorised the text as best he could, wrote it out, and sold it to a publisher who issued the mangled version as the genuine article. This is what happened in 1594 to *Henry VI,* Part 2, published as *The First Part of the Contention.* Plays were normally issued as quartos, a term describing the

The first illustration to Shakespeare: a production of *Titus Andronicus, c.* 1594

size of the printed page, and these corrupt texts have been given the name of 'bad' quartos. There are at least six Shakespearean 'bad' quartos, of which the most famous is *Hamlet*.

When times were bad the companies were driven to sell some of their stock, and in this manner *Titus Andronicus* found its way into the market, probably appearing just before 2 *Henry VI*, thus becoming the first of Shakespeare's plays to be published. For times were very bad in 1594. The plague had played havoc with the companies. The Earl of Pembroke's had to pawn their clothes, the Queen's were broken and became a second-rate troupe of provincial players, and the only companies to weather the storm were the Admiral's (that is, the company of Lord Admiral Howard who had commanded the fleet against the Armada) and the Earl of Derby's, formerly Lord Strange's. Derby died in the spring, but the company had found another patron in Lord Hunsdon who, as Lord Chamberlain, was responsible for the conduct of the theatres and the presentation of plays at Court. As he was also Elizabeth's favourite cousin they could scarcely have found a more promising patron.

The Lord Chamberlain's Servant
When the theatres reopened, therefore, Shakespeare's choice of companies was really limited to two. Though both would be more than eager to have him and his new plays he threw in his lot with the Chamberlain's, with whom he was to stay for the rest of his career. Other members of that immortal fellowship were John Heminge, apparently a former colleague of Shakespeare's with the Queen's, Augustine Phillips the musician, Will Kempe the celebrated dancer and comedian, Henry Condell and Richard Burbage, younger son of James Burbage, owner of the Theatre. So it was to the Theatre that the Chamberlain's went in the wet summer of 1594, while their rivals, the Admiral's, under

Will Kempe dancing a morris

The patron of Shakespeare's company, and two of its leading members

Lord Chamberlain Hunsdon

Richard Burbage,
who played Shakespeare's heroes.
Possibly a self-portrait

Edward Alleyn of the Admiral's company, who played Marlowe's tragic heroes

Henslowe and his new son-in-law Edward Alleyn, settled in again at the Rose on the other side of the river. Shakespeare took lodgings not far from the Theatre, in the neighbourhood of Bishopsgate.

He would find the theatrical scene strangely altered, for not only had the plague years quite transformed the actors' companies, they had also witnessed the virtual extinction of the men who had carried through the first stage of the dramatic revolution. Greene had died in 1592, a year later Marlowe had been killed in a brawl, and Kyd too was dead. Peele was dying, Lodge had turned adventurer and no longer wrote for the stage. Lyly had written nothing since the Paul's boys had ceased playing three years before, and Nashe was a pamphleteer rather than a playwright. At the age of thirty Shakespeare was left without rivals more formidable than Chettle and the 'peaking pageanter' Anthony Munday.

This was a serious position for Henslowe, now virtual owner of the Admiral's and their stock. Marlowe had been his man, and though he could go on producing his half-dozen plays he would have to find new men to supply new matter if he was to compete with Shakespeare and the Chamberlain's. His solution was a brilliant one from a commercial point of view. Less interested in quality than quantity and a rapid turnover of new plays, he set up a sort of dramatic workshop to which he enticed needy poets with the bait of steady

George Chapman, possibly the
rival poet of Shakespeare's *Sonnets*

The poet Michael Drayton,
Shakespeare's friend,
and a frequent visitor to Stratford

'Rare Ben Jonson', who 'loved Shakespeare, on this side idolatry, as much as any'

employment at a fixed, though admittedly not excessive, wage. In this way he attracted Munday and Chettle, and two of Shakespeare's contemporaries, Chapman and Drayton, true poets though with no particular aptitude for writing plays, and a number of younger men in their early twenties, a second generation as it were to replace the University Wits, including Thomas Heywood, Thomas Dekker, Ben Jonson and John Marston. Having collected his men he set them to work as a team in the mass-production of plays, each concentrating on what he could do best—tragedy, comedy, pathos, and so on. Munday, an ingenious spinner of plots, seems to have been in charge.

One of the plays manufactured by Munday and his men, or at least two of them, Chettle and Heywood, was *Sir Thomas More*, but when it went to the Master of the Revels to be licensed for production it was censored and returned for revision. Munday called in two more of his team to help, one being Dekker, and the other an unknown author who wrote three new pages describing More's pacification of a riot. These three pages are of profound importance, for the unknown author is thought by some scholars to be Shakespeare, and the writing to be his hand. If so, it is an invaluable aid to the correction of errors in the printed text of his plays, for we can understand the kind of mistake a printer might make when working from such a script, in which, for example, the letters *e, o* and *d* are easily confused. There is a strong case to be made for

A page from *Sir Thomas More*, possibly in Shakespeare's handwriting

Shakespeare's hand, but inevitably it depends mainly on a comparison with authentic specimens of his writing, and of these there are only six, all of them signatures made some twenty years later. Then, it seems in the highest degree unlikely that Shakespeare would help to revise an Admiral's play produced as a counterblast to his own work for the Chamberlain's.

That he really was a member of the Chamberlain's is proved by the record of his being one of the payees for the company, along with Kempe and Burbage, for two Court performances at Greenwich Palace at Christmas 1594. They were paid £6.13.4 for each performance and £3.6.8 'by way of Her Majesty's reward', the customary handsome tip from the Queen when she herself was present; £20 in all, or about £600 to-day, an enviable sum for distribution among eight sharers, even after paying for their costumes, their hirelings and boys. There would be few other expenses, as the Revels Office supplied any properties they needed, including the lath and canvas 'houses' that served as scenes, as in the medieval plays. One of their 'comedies or Enterludes' would almost certainly be *The Comedy of Errors,* which they presented on the following night in the hall of Gray's Inn. This was the Inn's 'Grand Night', when they entertained their neighbours from the Inner Temple, the festivities proving so riotous that on the next day a mock trial was held in which a sorcerer was found guilty of foisting on them 'a company of base and common Fellows to make up our disorders with a Play of Errors and Confusion'.

Although the Admiral's gave as many Court performances as the Chamberlain's that Christmas, they lost ground in the following year, and by 1596 were completely eclipsed, the Chamberlain's giving all six performances. Shakespeare's lyrical vein seemed inexhaustible, and comedy, tragedy and history flowed from his pen, all crammed with the splendid poetry of the sonnets. What had the Admiral's to offer against *Love's Labour's Lost, A Midsummer Night's Dream, Romeo and Juliet,* and *Richard II*? And how could they compete with such poetry as this?—

> *For Orpheus' lute was strung with poets' sinews*
> *Whose golden touch could soften steel and stones,*
> *Make tigers tame and huge leviathans*
> *Forsake unsounded deeps to dance on sands.*

Or this?

> *Death, that hath suck'd the honey of thy breath,*
> *Hath had no power yet upon thy beauty:*
> *Thou art not conquer'd; beauty's ensign yet*
> *Is crimson in thy lips and in thy cheeks,*
> *And death's pale flag is not advanced there.*

Payment to Kempe, Shakespeare and Burbage
for a performance at Greenwich Palace, Christmas 1594

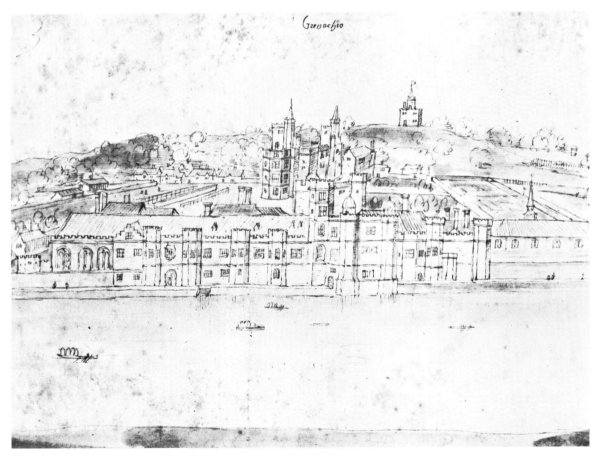

Greenwich Palace in 1594

The Hall of Gray's Inn, where
The Comedy of Errors was performed
in December 1594

But if Henslowe could not compete with the Chamberlain's at Court, he could at least provide his company and their audiences with a better theatre, and he spent more than £100 in painting and 'other repracyones' at the Rose. Such improvements and repairs were all the more necessary now that a rival had appeared on Bankside. This was Francis Langley, who in the course of 1595 built the 'finest and biggest' theatre in London, the Swan in Paris Garden, about a quarter of a mile further west.

Soon after its opening a Dutchman called de Witt saw a play there, and made a sketch. Unfortunately this has been lost, but a friend made a copy, and as this is our only contemporary illustration of the interior of an Elizabethan theatre it is of the first importance. Yet it must be treated with caution, for not only is it merely a copy, but the original drawing itself was no more than a sketch from memory, for if de Witt had been sitting in the theatre at the time he would not have drawn a bird's-eye view. However, it gives a good general

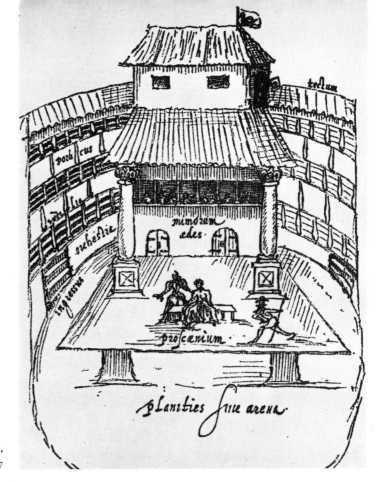

The Swan Theatre, built by Francis Langley, where Shakespeare and his company played in 1596-7

impression. Here are the galleries surrounding the arena with its apron stage, partly sheltered by a canopy or 'shadow' supported on pillars. At the back is the *mimorum aedes,* the actors' quarters or tiring-house, from which two doors lead on to the stage. Above these is a gallery in which apparently are spectators, and at the top is a hut, the medieval 'heavens', where thunder and other celestial —and terrestrial—noises were manufactured. Presumably there is another gallery, perhaps for musicians, hidden by the canopy. The most puzzling feature is the absence of an upper stage, if the people in the gallery really are spectators and not actors, and of a small curtained stage below. By this time, when plays were no longer acrobatic entertainments, the 'groundlings' who stood in the bottom gallery may have been turned into the yard, to the great profit of the players, and it is now that we first hear of gallants hiring stools to sit on the stage itself.

The Chamberlain's would be as interested as Henslowe in Langley's venture, though for another reason. The lease of the land on which the Theatre stood was running out, and if Burbage failed to get a renewal on reasonable terms, as seemed probable, the Swan would be a welcome alternative.

Stratford Affairs   So matters stood in the summer of 1596, when Shakespeare received news that his son, Hamnet, was desperately ill. Perhaps the boy died before he could reach Stratford, though it is impossible to read *King John*, which he was then writing, without finding a reflection of his anguish as he took the little body in his arms, in the line of Faulconbridge watching Hubert lift the body of the boy Arthur, 'How easy dost thou take all England up!' For Hamnet was his only son, all England to him in his grief. He was only eleven.

Yet so much remained. His wife Anne, it is true, was now forty, eight years his senior, and perhaps no very congenial companion for a poet accustomed to the life of London and the Court. But there was Hamnet's twin, Judith, and her sister Susanna, two years older. Then, his father and mother were still alive, and with them his sister and three brothers, for they were all as yet unmarried, Edmund, the youngest, being not much older than Hamnet. The Henley Street house was getting decidedly small for such a family, particularly since the great fires of the last two years, when one end had to be pulled down to prevent its catching alight. It had been a disastrous period, for more than two hundred buildings had been destroyed, most of them at the upper end of the town, and many of the Shakespeares' friends, including the Quineys and Sturleys, had been left homeless. But the new houses were going up, the finest being that of the bailiff, wealthy Thomas Rogers, in High Street.

When John Shakespeare had been bailiff, nearly thirty years before, eager in his prosperity to gentle his condition he had applied for a grant of arms, but during his years of adversity had had no heart to pursue the matter. Now that his fortunes had been restored, thanks to his successful son, he renewed the claim; for though Hamnet was dead, he had four sons, and the chances were that there would be other grandsons to inherit the rank of gentleman. A few months earlier William would have been as eager as his father, but now it must

The Stratford house built by Thomas Rogers, Shakespeare's neighbour and grandfather of John Harvard ▶

The Grant of Arms
to John Shakespeare

have seemed something of a vanity; yet there were Susanna and Judith to be considered, his brothers too, and he himself was not without ambition. So the application was made, and in October John Shakespeare, gentleman, was granted a coat of arms: 'Gould, on a bend sable, a speare of the first steeled argent. And for his creast or cognizaunce a faulcon, his wings displayed Argent standing on a wrethe of his coullers, supporting a speare gould steeled as aforesaid.'

Shakespeare was in no hurry to leave Stratford, for as the Chamberlain's were on tour there was no reason why he should return to London before they began rehearsals for the Revels, and perhaps it was during his protracted stay that he began the almost cynical and heartless *Merchant of Venice,* the last of the lyrical plays, in which his early poetry reaches perfection. When at length he did return he found the affairs of his company in some confusion. Lord Huns, don had died, and though his son had agreed to become their patron he was not the new Lord Chamberlain. This was Lord Cobham, no friend of the players, and the City Corporation made the most of their golden opportunity. They had failed to prevent the building of the Swan, according to them merely another place of meeting for 'theeves, horsestealers, whoremoongers, coozeners, connycatching persones, practizers of treason & such other lyke', but now they succeeded in persuading Cobham and the Privy Council to close the inn-theatres in the City. This was a severe blow, as the Chamberlain's used the Cross Keys in the winter, when the Theatre and Curtain proved too far afield, the way too miry, for London's citizens. So they came to terms with Langley, booked the Swan for the

Shakespeare's new patron, the second Lord Chamberlain Hunsdon

winter season, and Shakespeare moved his lodgings from Bishopsgate to Bankside. His association with Langley was soon to involve him in a quarrel.

Langley was on the worst of terms with one of the local Surrey magistrates, William Gardiner, whom he had publicly denounced, apparently with every justification, as 'a false perjured knave', scarcely a conciliatory phrase. The furious Gardiner thereupon enlisted the aid of his worthless stepson, William Wayte, and the two so threatened Langley that he sought legal protection from them, 'for fear of death, and so forth'. The danger was a real one in those turbulent days of swaggering gallants, when swords were light in their sheaths and constables as discreet as Dogberry. Marlowe had been had up for murder before he was himself killed with a dagger, and Jonson narrowly escaped hanging for running through a fellow actor with his sword. Gardiner would stick at nothing, and as a magistrate would certainly do his best to ruin Langley

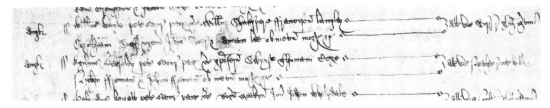

William Wayte craves sureties of the peace against William Shakspere and Francis Langley

Sir Thomas Lucy, buried in Charlecote church, 1600

by closing the Swan. No doubt this was why Shakespeare came to his aid, and why Wayte in his turn craved sureties of the peace against 'William Shakspere, Francis Langley' and two unknown women, Dorothy Soer and Anne Lee. Evidently Shakespeare was a dangerous opponent, though if Gardiner was the original of Justice Shallow he was a generous one, for the satire is nothing like as ferocious as that rascally magistrate deserved. But perhaps the fussy and ineffectual Shallow was a caricature of his Stratford neighbour and traditional persecutor, Sir Thomas Lucy.

He could not resist a hit at Lord Cobham, the man who had closed the Cross Keys to him and his company, and in his next play, *Henry IV,* gave the fat and uncourageous knight the name of his ancestor, Sir John Oldcastle. Cobham protested, and, to the great delight of his numerous enemies, Shakespeare changed the name to Falstaff, another historical character with a kind of alacrity in running away. The name stuck, and thenceforth Cobham was facetiously known as Falstaff. Shakespeare had his revenge. But in the spring of 1597 Lord Chamberlain Cobham died, unwept of the players, and to the great joy of Shakespeare and his fellows, their patron, the second Lord Hunsdon, was appointed to the vacant office. Once more they were the Lord Chamberlain's men.

Shortly after this Shakespeare was in Stratford again. He had money to invest, and like his father prudently put it into property. For some time he had had his eye on New Place, the 'praty howse of brike and tymber' opposite the Gild Chapel and his old school. The owner was William Underhill, 'a covetous and crafty man' who stood out for a stiff price, and in May Shakespeare paid him £60 for the house with its two barns, two gardens and two orchards. A few weeks later Underhill was poisoned by his crazy son.

There were repairs to be done, for the house was in poor condition, and the two parts of *Henry IV* are full of images that reveal Shakespeare's preoccupation with building—'The frame and huge foundation of the earth', 'like one that draws the model of a house', and so on. More prosaically, he sold a ton of stone to the Corporation for the repair of Clopton bridge, perhaps the remains of one of his tumbledown barns. This was his first house, and his delight in ordinary domestic occupations is reflected in the homely imagery that character

The house that Shakespeare bought in Stratford: New Place, 'a praty howse of brike and tymber'

ises the plays of this period, and indeed all his later work: 'Knit our powers to the arm of peace', 'like the bees, culling from every flower', for undoubtedly there were bees in the long-neglected garden that he was putting in order:

> He cannot so precisely weed this land . . .
> His foes are so enrooted with his friends
> That, plucking to unfix an enemy,
> He doth unfasten so and shake a friend.

And when he looked up from his gardening in the afternoon he saw the school-boys running 'east, west, north, south' along the crossroads at his corner, and naturally described the dispersal of an army as 'like a school broke up, Each hurries toward his home and sporting-place'—very different from their snail-like morning crawl, equally observed. His heart must have ached. Hamnet should have been among them.

The Middle Comedies

The death of Hamnet had a profound effect on Shakespeare, both as man and artist. He did not turn to tragic themes as a lesser man might have done; on the contrary, the plays of the next few years are the most seeming-happy of all. But there is a new mellowness and compassion, an extension of sympathy and understanding to characters of all classes and all ages. He was no longer a somewhat self-centred lover and poet identifying himself almost exclusively with the lovers and poets in his plays, but a dramatist with a passionate interest in all people, and the change was reflected in his style. The old lyrical elation was subdued and these historical and romantic comedies, from *Henry IV* to *Twelfth Night*, were written in a language much closer to that really spoken by men than anything that had gone before. We have only to compare the end of *The Merchant of Venice* with the opening of *Henry IV* to see the transition from the lovely but undramatic lyricism to a more natural and dramatic verse. Here is the Venetian Lorenzo:

> The moon shines bright: in such a night as this,
> When the sweet wind did gently kiss the trees
> And they did make no noise, in such a night
> Troilus methinks mounted the Troyan walls,
> And sighed his soul toward the Grecian tents,
> Where Cressid lay that night.

And here the English Harry:

> So shaken as we are, so wan with care,
> Find we a time for frighted peace to pant,
> And breathe short-winded accents of new broils
> To be commenced in strands afar remote.

All that remains of New Place ▶

The earlier plays had been mainly in verse, often in rhyme, and prose had been reserved for comic characters, significantly enough more memorable than most of the verse speakers, for lyric poetry is not the stuff of which men and women are made. But the plays of this group were for the most part written in prose, which now became the speech of kings as well as clowns, and out of it Shakespeare created many of his most lovable characters—Falstaff, Benedick, Beatrice and Rosalind. In short, lyric poetry gave way to dramatic prose, as dramatic prose was in turn to lead up to dramatic poetry.

It seems probable that after buying New Place Shakespeare no longer went on tour with his company, but whenever he could spent the summer in Stratford with his family. It would certainly pay the Chamberlain's handsomely to give their dramatist time to write the plays on which their prosperity so largely depended, and he is not likely to have demurred at such an arrangement. So we may imagine him settling into New Place in the summer of 1597 with his wife and two young daughters, writing *Henry IV*, and perhaps finding time to attend the wedding of his sister Joan, which probably took place somewhere in the neighbourhood of Stratford. Her husband was William Hart, a hatter, and the couple took over the rooms in the Henley Street house vacated by the family at New Place.

On his return to London Shakespeare found that there had been disturbing developments in his absence. Old James Burbage had died, and his sons Cuthbert and Richard had been unable to renew the lease of the land on which the Theatre stood. To make matters more difficult, Langley had got into trouble in July for allowing the Earl of Pembroke's players to produce a satirical comedy, *The Isle of Gulls*, at the Swan. On the grounds that it contained 'very seditious and sclanderous matter' the Privy Council ordered the closing of all the theatres, the imprisonment of some of the players and of the authors, one of whom was Nashe, who escaped, and the other Ben Jonson. Then when the general ban was lifted in October Langley was refused a renewal of his licence for the Swan as a theatre, and had to turn it into a sort of circus. Evidently Gardiner too had his revenge. This meant that the Theatre, Swan, and City inns were all closed to the Chamberlain's, while the Rose, of course, was occupied by the Admiral's. The only other theatre was the Curtain, not easily accessible in winter, and for the time being the Chamberlain's had to be content with this old and second-rate house.

Perhaps it was to help tide over this difficult period that they sold four of Shakespeare's plays to the publishers in 1597-98: *Richard II, Richard III, 1 Henry IV,* and *Love's Labour's Lost,* the first play to be published with his name. It should be noted that Shakespeare himself did not sell to the publishers, and had little control therefore over their production, the quality of which varied with the

A PLEASANT Conceited Comedie CALLED, Loues labors loft.

As it vvas prefented before her Highnes this laft Chriftmas.

Newly corrected and augmented By *W. Shakefpere.*

Imprinted at London by *W.W.* for *Cutbert Burby.* 1598.

The first play to be published with Shakespeare's name

printer; William White, for example, made a poor job of the *Love's Labour's Lost* quarto, while Valentine Simmes produced a relatively good text of *Richard II*, though even he made 69 errors, and when he printed a second edition, after correcting 14, added 123 new ones. Plays simply were not treated as serious literature, and the best printers did not deal in them, and though Shakespeare might have insisted on seeing proofs, he was incurably easy-going and too deeply absorbed in what he was writing to trouble himself overmuch about what he had written.

Not everybody, however, took such a contemptuous view of plays as the stationers. In September, 1598, a schoolmaster called Francis Meres published his *Palladis Tamia: Wit's Treasury*, one section of which is a fantastic attempt to find classical parallels for contemporary English poets. As criticism it is quite valueless, but for the information that it gives about Shakespeare it is beyond price. It needed no 'Maister of Artes of both Universities' to tell us that he was considered the best dramatist of the day, both for comedy and tragedy, but only an intelligent contemporary in touch with writers and the theatre could have

mong al writers to be of an honeſt life and
vpright conuerſation:ſo *Michael Drayton*
(quē toties honoris & amoris cauſa nomino)
among ſchollers,ſouldiours,Poets, and all
ſorts of people,is helde for a man of vertuous diſpoſition,honeſt conuerſation , and
wel gouerned cariage,which is almoſt mi-
raculous among good wits in theſe decli-
ning and corrupt times, when there is nothing but rogery in villanous man, & whē
cheating and craftines is counted the clea-
neſt wit, and ſoundeſt wiſedome.

As *Decius Auſonius Gallus in libris Fa-
ſtorum*,penned the occurrences of ȳ world
from the firſt creation of it to his time,that
is,to the raigne of the Emperor *Gratian*:ſo
Warner in his abſolute *Albions Englande*
hath moſt admirably penned the hiſtorie
of his own country from *Noah* to his time,
that is,to the raigne of Queene *Elizabeth*,
I haue heard him termd the beſt wits of
both our Vniuerſities,our Engliſh *Homer*.

As *Euripedes* is the moſt ſententious a-
mong the Greek Poets:ſo is *Warner* amōg
our Engliſh Poets.

As the ſoule of *Euphorbus* was thought
to liue in *Pythagoras* : ſo the ſweete wittie
ſoule of *Ouid* liues in mellifluous & hony-
tongued *Shakeſpeare*,witnes his *Venus* and
Adonis,his *Lucrece* , his ſugred Sonnets
among

among his priuate friends,&c.

As *Plautus* and *Seneca* are accounted
the beſt for Comedy and Tragedy among
the Latines : ſo *Shakeſpeare* among ȳ Engliſh is the moſt excellent in both kinds for
the ſtage;for Comedy, witnes his *Gētlemē
of Verona*,his *Errors*,his *Loue labors loſt*,his
Loue labours wonne,his *Midſummers night
dreame*,& his *Merchant of Venice*:for Tragedy his *Richard the 2.Richard the 3.Hen-
ry the 4.King Iohn*,*Titus Andronicus* and
his *Romeo* and *Iuliet*.

As *Epius Stolo* ſaid,that the Muſes would
ſpeake with *Plautus* tongue,if they would
ſpeak Latin:ſo I ſay that the Muſes would
ſpeak with *Shakeſpeares* fine filed phraſe,if
they would ſpeake Engliſh.

As *Muſæus*,who wrote the loue of *Hero*
and *Leander*,had two excellent ſchollers,
Thamaras & *Hercules*:ſo hath he in England two excelent Poets,imitators of him
in the ſame argument and ſubiect,*Chriſto-
pher Marlow*,and *George Chapman*.

As *Ouid* ſaith of his worke;
*Iamᵹ opus exegi,quod nec Iouis ira,nec ignis,
Nec poterit ferrum,nec edax abolere vetuſtas,*

And as Horace ſaith of his;*Exegi monu-
nentū ære perennius;Regaliᵹ,ſitu pyramidū
uod non imber edax; Non Aquilo
oſſit diruere; aut innumerabilis*
O o 2. *annorum*

'Hony-tongued Shakespeare': a contemporary opinion

told us that his sonnets were then circulating among his friends, and recorded
twelve of the plays that he had written. Meres had a pedantic passion for balance
in his prose—six comedies set against six tragedies—which may account for his
omission of the three parts of *Henry VI*, and his not inappropriate title of
'Loue labours wonne' for, presumably, *The Taming of the Shrew*.

Palladis Tamia was fresh from the press when the Chamberlain's opened their
autumn season at the Curtain with Jonson's first important comedy, *Every Man
in his Humour*. There is a tradition that Shakespeare was responsible for his
company's acceptance of the play; certainly he acted in it, and Jonson's list of
the 'principall comœdians', appended later to the collected edition of his
Works, is the first definite record of his acting, and incidentally the first complete
cast of the company. Condell and Sly were now full adventurers, but Beeston
and Duke were hirelings, and never became sharers. The play was a portent,
a realistic comedy with a purpose, and a revolt against the romantic plays of
Shakespeare, of which Jonson made fun in his Prologue. Shakespeare replied
in *As You Like It* with a genial sketch of Jonson as the 'humorous' Jaques,

whose ambition was to 'cleanse the foul body of the infected world'. The two had little in common except genius, the one arrogant, pushing and intolerant, the other all sympathy for his fellow men, never making his work a vehicle for propaganda.

We have an example of Shakespeare's generosity at this very time. His friends, Adrian Quiney and his son Richard, had been badly hit by the fires at Stratford, and when Richard was in London shortly after the production of *Every Man in his Humour*, he wrote to Shakespeare urgently asking for a loan of £30 to help them out of their difficulties. Shakespeare lost no time in replying, or possibly went at once to see him at his lodging near St. Paul's, for on the same day Richard wrote home to say that his 'countryman' had promised them the money. It is the only fragment that remains of Shakespeare's correspondence.

There were other pressing claims upon his purse that winter. The Chamber- *The Globe* lain's had no intention of staying indefinitely at the Curtain, and after careful *Theatre* consideration had selected a site for a new theatre on Bankside, almost—to Henslowe's horror—opposite the Rose. On the 26th they played before the

This Comoedie was firſt
Acted, in the yeere
1 5 9 8.

By the then L. Chamberlayne
his Seruants.

The principall Comœdians were.

Will Shakespeare. ⎱ Ric. Bvrbadge.
Avg. Philips. ⎰ Ioh. Hemings.
Hen. Condel. ⎱ Tho. Pope.
Will. Slye. ⎰ Chr. Beeston.
Will. Kempe. Ioh. Dvke.

Cast of the first performance
of Ben Jonson's *Every Man in his Humour*

With the allowance of the Maſter of Revells.

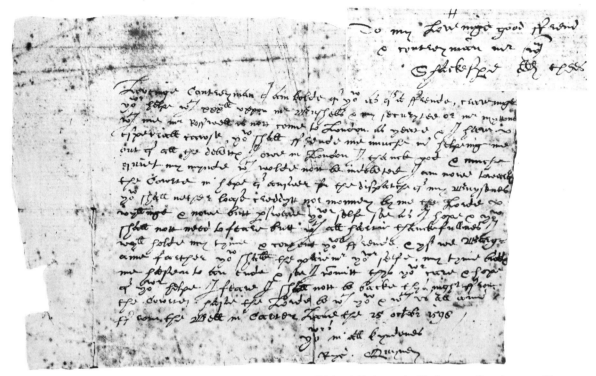

Richard Quiney asks Shakespeare for a loan, 25 Oct. 1598

Queen at Whitehall, and two days later carried out the audacious raid that they had been planning for some time. Although the Theatre was now on alien ground, it belonged, according to their interpretation of the lease, to the Burbage brothers, so arming themselves with axes they invaded the precinct and under the skilled direction of Peter Street, a carpenter, began its demolition. Then, as their opponents put it, 'they did in most forcible and ryotous manner take and carrye away from thence all the wood and timber'. There was a deal of wood and timber in the Theatre, and it must have been a strange sight to see Shakespeare and his companions trundling balks and beams along Bishopsgate, and over London Bridge to Bankside. There, on the marshy ground opposite the Rose, Street built another theatre for them. They called it the Globe, their sign being Hercules bearing the earth on his shoulders, symbol perhaps of their Herculean labour.

Street used what he could of the salvaged timber, but some of it was in poor condition, and the new Globe was by no means the old Theatre set up on a new site. The plays of 1599 were very different from those of 1576, for which James Burbage had prepared to cater before the dramatic revolution, and Shakespeare and his fellows knew from long experience exactly what they

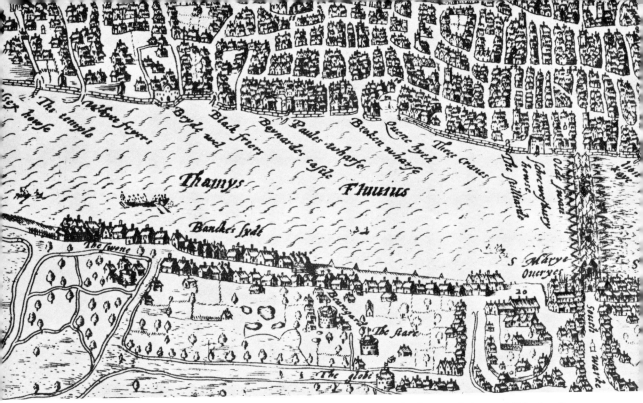

The newly built Globe, opposite the Rose (misnamed 'The Stare')

wanted. Of course the audience must be made as comfortable as possible, but it was the stage that mattered. All the paraphernalia of trapdoors communicating with 'hell' beneath the apron stage were there, as well as corresponding quaint devices in the 'heavens', whence aerial visitations could be made. But the essential thing was the provision of a fully developed upper stage, projecting over the apron on the level of the middle gallery, and beneath this a curtained lower stage, which could be used to disclose more formal indoor scenes. Thus, with three stages and two levels, and the use of the yard if required, the most exacting of Shakespeare's plays could be produced, the action flowing un-broken over the whole of the playing-place. It was for this 'wooden O' that Shakespeare began to write *Henry V,* a history that would tax its resources to the utmost.

The Chamberlain's had now added a theatre to their common stock. Ten shares were created, half of them being allotted to the Burbage brothers, who had contributed the fabric of their Theatre, and the other five to those members of the company who paid for the building. Shakespeare was one of them—indeed, the Globe was described soon after its opening as 'a playhouse occupied by William Shakespeare and others'—so that to the income he earned as

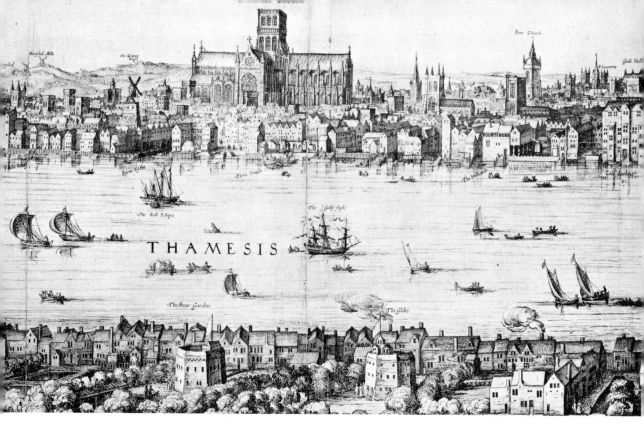

Bankside, where Shakespeare lived for many years

dramatist and actor he now added a tenth of the profits derived from the theatre itself. As dramatist he would receive about £10 for each play, as actor he was entitled to one eighth of the money paid for standing room and half that paid for seats in the galleries, as theatre-owner, or 'householder', to one tenth of the other half of the gallery takings. In addition there were the substantial rewards for Court performances. By the beginning of the new century his income was probably the equivalent of about £5,000 of our money, virtually free from tax. No wonder the actors at the Rose, all of them in debt to Henslowe, whose deliberate policy it was thus to keep them in his clutches, looked enviously at the free and prosperous association over the way, and Henslowe himself began to look about for another site for a theatre as far away from the Globe as possible.

While Shakespeare and his companions were dismantling the Theatre, Spenser had arrived in London, a refugee from Ireland, where his home had been sacked and burned by the rebels. He died a month later, apparently in poverty, and was buried in Westminster Abbey. Ireland was ablaze with rebellion, and the ambitious, unpredictable Essex persuaded the Queen to send him to extinguish it. In March he set out at the head of an army, taking with

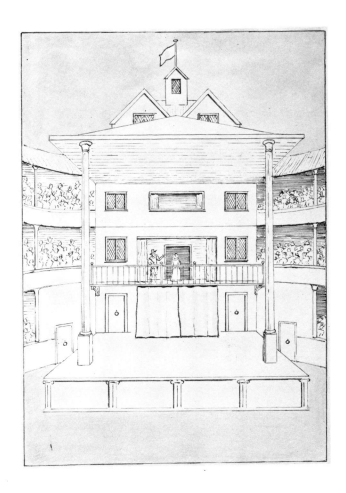

A reconstruction of the Globe stage

him the Earl of Southampton as General of the Horse, and Shakespeare, nearing the end of *Henry V*, wrote:

> *Were now the general of our gracious empress,*
> *As in good time he may, from Ireland coming,*
> *Bringing rebellion broached on his sword,*
> *How many would the peaceful city quit*
> *To welcome him!*

But Essex did no such thing. After wasting the summer in futile marches he lost his nerve, made a truce with Tyrone, the rebel leader, deserted his army, and threw himself on Elizabeth's mercy. She placed him under arrest, and though soon released he was a discredited and ruined man, exiled from her favour and the Court. A dangerous man at this critical time, the old Queen's cousin and the people's darling, and the succession to the throne still unsettled.

Henry V was probably the play with which the Globe was opened in the

The first entry of Shakespeare's name in the
Stationers' Register

golden Legacie;

vp in his armes hee threw him against the grounde so violently,
that hee broake his necke, and so ended his dayes with his brother. At this vnlookt for massacre, the people murmured, and
were all in a deepe passion of pittie, but the Francklin, father
vnto these, neuer chaunged his countenance, but as a man of a
couragious resolution, tooke vp the bodies of his sonnes without shewe of outward discontent.

All this while stood Rosader and sawe this Tragedie : who
noting the vndoubted vertue of the Francklins minde, alighted of
from his Horse, and presently sat downe on the grasse, and commanded his boy to pul off his bootes, making him ready to try the
strength of this Champion, being furnished as he would, he clapt
the Francklin on the shoulder and said thus, Bold yeoman whose
sonnes haue ended the tearme of their yeares with honour, for
that I see thou scornest fortune with patience, and rewardest the
iniurp of fate with content, in brooking the death of thy sonnes :
stand a while and either see me make a third in their Tragedie, or
else reuenge their fal with an honourable triumph, the Francklin
seeing so goodly a gentleman to giue him such curteous comfort,
gaue him hartie thankes, with promise to pray for his happy suc-
cesse. With that Rosader vailed bonnet to the King, and lightly
leapt within the lists, where noting more the companie then the
combataunt, hee cast his eye vpon the troupe of Ladies that glitte-
red there lyke the starres of heauen, but at last Loue willing to
make him as amorous as hee was valiaunt, presented him
with the sight of Rosalynd, whose admirable beautie so in-
veagled the eye of Rosader, that forgetting himselfe, hee stoode
and fedde his lookes on the fauour of Rosalyndes face, which
thee perceiuing, blusht : which was such a doubling of her beau-
teous excellence, that the bashful redde of Aurora, at the sight of
vnacquainted Phaeton, was not halfe so glorious :

The Normane seeing this young Gentleman fettered
in the lookes of the Ladyes, draue him out of his memen-
to with a shake by the shoulder : Rosader looking backe with
an angrie frowne, as if hee had been wakened from some plea-
saunt dreame, discouered to all by the furye of his countenance that hee was a man of some high thoughts ; but when they

C 2   ail

The source of *As You Like It*

autumn of 1599, soon after Essex's disgrace. Shakespeare himself must have played the part of Chorus, and though in his Prologue he apologised for the new theatre's inadequacy for the presentation of 'so great an object', we can sense the pride he felt at introducing his audience to its girdling walls. He took no part in *Every Man out of his Humour*, which followed soon afterwards, a confused and tedious play, in which Jonson incidentally made game of Shakespeare's new gentility and motto, *Non sans droit*, by suggesting as an alternative *Not without mustard*.

The Chamberlain's had to raise money for the building of the Globe by selling some of their stock, and in 1600 offered four of Shakespeare's plays to the publishers: *The Merchant of Venice, A Midsummer Night's Dream, Much Ado about Nothing,* and *2 Henry IV.* All were duly entered in the Stationers' Register, the last two together, a particularly interesting entry, for it is the first in which Shakespeare's name is recorded. A few days earlier the company had discovered that one of their hirelings had vamped up a version of *Henry V* with the intention of turning a dishonest penny by selling it to a stationer. They did their best to prevent publication, but it was no good, and the mutilated version joined the 'bad' quartos of 2, 3 *Henry VI* and *Romeo and Juliet* in the booksellers' shops near St. Paul's. *The Merry Wives of Windsor,* written at about this time, was soon to make a fifth.

Although Shakespeare was gradually being relieved of his duties as an actor, it was a particularly busy period for him. He was writing hard to supply the Globe with new plays that would make the venture a success, and help to pay off the loans they had been compelled to take up at a high rate of interest. Somehow in the course of 1599-1600 he managed to produce *Julius Caesar,* and *As You Like It,* based on Thomas Lodge's romance, *Rosalynde,* with music by Thomas Morley, and by the Christmas of 1600 he had a third play ready for the Revels. This was *Twelfth Night,* presented in the great hall of Whitehall Palace on Twelfth Night, 1601, as a compliment to Elizabeth's distinguished guest, the young Italian nobleman, Virginio Orsino, Duke of Bracciano. As a compliment to Elizabeth as well, who was expected to identify herself with Olivia, for according to the fiction of the Court she was still the Faery Queen against whose youth and beauty time was powerless. She was, in fact, sixty-eight, black-toothed, red-wigged and wrinkled. Nor was Shakespeare under any illusion about the destructive power of time. It is indeed a constant theme in his early poetry: 'wasteful time', 'devouring time', 'cormorant time'. Up till now he had seen age from the side of youth, but *Twelfth Night* is a transition, a reconciliation with time, an acceptance of the fact that he himself was no longer young, and henceforth he saw youth with compassionate eyes from the side of age. It is the last, as it is the most perfect, of his middle comedies.

Thomas Morley's setting of a Shakespeare song, from his *First Booke of Ayres,* 1600

Exactly a month later, on Friday, February 6th, half a dozen gentlemen called at the Globe and asked the Chamberlain's to put on a special performance of Shakespeare's *Richard II* the next day. They demurred, protesting that it was an old play that would attract but a poor audience. When they were offered forty shillings, however, they agreed, and on the Saturday afternoon played the tragedy of the deposing and killing of King Richard to a disappointed audience. The next morning three hundred armed men poured out of Essex House in the Strand, and headed by the Earl stormed up Ludgate and along Cheapside,

Ben Jonson gives Marston a pill

calling on the citizens to 'liberate' the Queen from her evil counsellors. Not a man joined them. The desperate Essex surrendered, and the rest of the leaders, including Southampton, were arrested. Ten days later they were brought to trial, found guilty of treason, and condemned to death, though Southampton's sentence was commuted to life imprisonment. On the 25th the old Queen's young favourite was executed at the Tower. The Chamberlain's had been unwittingly implicated in the rising, for the performance of *Richard II* was part of the plot—to remind the citizens that sovereigns might be deposed. They were questioned but found innocent, and on the eve of Essex's execution performed again at Whitehall.

The Admiral's gave three Court performances that Christmas, but they were no longer at the Rose. They had left Bankside to the Chamberlain's and moved over the river to Finsbury, north of Cripplegate, where Henslowe and Alleyn had built a fine new theatre, the Fortune, modelled on the Globe, though square in plan. More significant was the appearance, or reappearance, of two more companies at Court—the Children of Paul's and the Children of the Chapel. Shakespeare had never had to face the competition of the boys, for it was ten years since last they had been players. The Chamberlain's however, were themselves largely responsible for the venture. Before he died James Burbage had converted part of the Blackfriars buildings into a second private theatre, forming a hall some seventy feet long and fifty wide, equipped with a stage, galleries and seats. Protests from the residents had prevented his opening it, but in 1600 his sons leased it to the Master of the Chapel Children, and performances began again. Here was something new to tickle the jaded palates of the citizens, and they flocked to Blackfriars and the singing-school of Paul's. Though their choirmasters could not command the pen of Shakespeare, who wrote exclusively for his own company, they commissioned the best of the other dramatists, and so began the profitable War of the Theatres—profitable that is, for the boys, though not so for the adult companies.

Ben Jonson and John Marston were quarrelsome young

men with different ideas about the drama. In *Every Man out of his Humour* Jonson had parodied Marston's bombastic style, and Marston had replied by pillorying Jonson in one of the first plays given by the Paul's boys. Jonson countered with *Cynthia's Revels*, written for the Chapel, in which both Marston and his friend Dekker were ridiculed. Again Marston hit back in a Paul's play. London was delighted, and all agog to see what would happen next. They were not disappointed. In the autumn of 1601 the Chapel Children played Jonson's *Poetaster,* satirising Dekker as the playdresser Demetrius and Marston as the poetaster Crispinus. The two are arraigned before Caesar, and Jonson, as the virtuous Horace, gives Crispinus a pill to make him vomit up his windy words. A few weeks later came the reply of Dekker and Marston in *Satiromastix,* produced at Paul's. The arrogant Horace is hauled up before—of all people—William Rufus, and Demetrius and Crispinus are appointed his judges. They prefer not to give him pills, fearing the stench of the black insolence they would fetch up, but crown him with nettles and make him swear to abandon his exhibitionism and conceit. Jonson would have replied, but he had offended the government by satirising more than rival playwrights, and was silenced. It was the last round in the War of the Theatres.

At Cambridge that Christmas the undergraduates played an anonymous comedy called *The Return from Parnassus,* in which Kempe and Burbage are introduced praising their colleague Shakespeare who had taken the bumptious Jonson down a peg or two. But what Shakespeare had to do with the War of the Theatres, and what was the purge he gave Jonson is a mystery, though he did add a footnote to the squabble and the competition of the 'aery of children' in *Hamlet,* which he was then writing.

The returne from Pernassus.

Kempe Its true indeede, honeſt *Dick*, but the ſlaues are ſomewhat proud, and beſides, it is a good ſport in a part, to ſee them neuer ſpeake in their walke, but at the end of the Ɽage, iuſt as though in walking with a fellow we ſhould neuer ſpeake but at a ſtile, a gate, or a ditch, where a man can go no further. I was once at a Comedie in Cambridge, and there I ſaw a paraſite make faces and mouths of all ſorts on this faſhion.

Bur. A little teaching will mend theſe faults, and it may bee beſides they will be able to pen a part.

Kemp. Few of the vniuerſity pen plaies well, they ſmell too much of that writer *Ouid*, and that writer *Metamorphoſis*, and talke too much of *Proſerpina & Iuppiter*. Why heres our fellow *Shakeſpeare* puts them all downe, I and *Ben Ionſon* too. O that *Ben Ionſon* is a peſtilent fellow, he brought vp *Horace* giuing the Poets a pill, but our fellow *Shakeſpeare* hath giuen him a purge that made him beray his credit:

Bur. Its a ſhrewd fellow indeed: I wonder theſe ſchollers ſtay ſo long, they appointed to be here preſẽtly that we might try them: oh here they come.

Stud. Take heart, theſe lets our clouded thoughts refine,
The ſun ſhines brighteſt when it gins decline.

Bur.M.Phil. and *M.Stud.* God ſaue you.

Kemp. M.*Phil.* and M.*Otioſo*, well met,

Phil The ſame to you good M. *Burbage.* What M. *Kempe*

What was the purge that Shakespeare gave Jonson?

Prince of Denmarke.

We boorded them a the way: they are comming to you.

Ham. Players, what Players be they?

Roſſ. My Lord, the Tragedians of the Citty,
Thoſe that you tooke delight to ſee ſo often.   (ſtie?

Ham. How comes it that they trauell? Do they grow re-

Gil. No my Lord, their reputation holds as it was wont.

Ham. How then?

Gil. Yfaith my Lord, noueltie carries it away,
For the principall publike audience that
Came to them, are turned to priuate playes,
And to the humour of children.

Ham. I doe not greatly wonder of it,
For thoſe that would make mops and moes
At my vncle, when my father liued,
Now giue a hundred, two hundred pounds
For his picture: but they ſhall be welcome,
He that playes the King ſhall haue tribute of me,
The ventrous Knight ſhall vſe his foyle and target,
The louer ſhall ſigh gratis,
The clowne ſhall make them laugh   (for't,
That are tickled in the lungs, or the blanke verſe ſhall halt
And the Lady ſhall haue leaue to ſpeake her minde freely.

The Trumpets ſound,   Enter Corambis.

Shakespeare's comment on 'The War of the Theatres', from the first, the 'bad', quarto of *Hamlet,* 1603

The Old Stratford estate bought by Shakespeare in 1602

'This Indenture . . . Betweene . . . John Combe of Old Stretford . . .
And William Shakespere of Stretford vppon Avon . . . gentleman . . .'

He may have missed the climax of the wordy warfare, for his father had died in September, and presumably he was in Stratford for the funeral, or soon afterwards. Perhaps the 'merry cheeked old man' had been attended in his last illness by the young Bedfordshire doctor, John Hall, who had just begun to practise in the town. There were other changes in the Henley Street house. His sister Joan had recently given birth to a son, his first nephew, and his youngest brother, Edmund, had left Stratford to become, like him, a player. But his other brothers were still there, and it was to Gilbert that he assigned the business of negotiating the purchase of an estate from William Combe and his nephew John, 127 acres of agricultural land in Old Stratford, just to the north of the town. By the spring of 1602, therefore, Shakespeare was a landed gentleman with the finest house in Stratford. Moreover he was at the height of his powers, and on the threshold of his greatest achievements.

Elizabeth, however, was failing. After the Christmas Revels the Court moved up the river to Richmond where, on February 2nd, 1603, the Chamberlain's presented a play, possibly the recently completed *Hamlet*. If so, nothing could have been more appropriate, for Shakespeare never saw the Queen again, and he had made his farewell:

> *Good night, sweet prince,*
> *And flights of angels sing thee to thy rest!*

She died in the early morning of March 24th.

Richmond Palace, where Queen Elizabeth died, 24 March 1603

James I and VI

The Chamberlain's become the King's Men, 19 May 1603

Another and less heroic age had dawned. The new sovereign was James, King of Scotland, a well-meaning but obstinate, pedantic man of about Shakespeare's age, his Queen an extravagant Danish princess, the mother of his three young children, Henry, Elizabeth and Charles. James lost no time in re-arranging his Court after his own liking, advancing his supporters and discarding his opponents. Lord Burghley's son, Robert Cecil, was confirmed as chief minister and soon created Earl of Salisbury, Francis Bacon was knighted, Shakespeare's patron, Southampton, released from prison, and Raleigh committed to the Tower. The reorganisation of Court life soon involved theatrical affairs, and within two months of his accession James had taken Shakespeare and his fellows under his own patronage. This change of patrons did not in itself involve any change of fortune, for though they were Grooms of the Chamber equipped with the royal scarlet livery, they were unpaid, as their office was merely an honorary one. The change of sovereigns, however, did involve a change of fortune. Under Elizabeth an average of six or seven Court performances had been given each year, under James there were rarely less than twenty, and as the King's Men gave the majority of these it meant a considerable increase in their incomes. All the other London companies were taken under royal patronage. The Admiral's became Prince Henry's, a new company playing at the Curtain became Queen Anne's, and the Chapel Children at Blackfriars were now known as the Children of the Queen's Revels.

At the beginning of this new era Shakespeare was just thirty-nine. It was exactly ten years since his first work had been published, ten years since Marlowe had died, and in the course of that astonishing decade the 'upstart crow' had written some twenty plays, from *Love's Labour's Lost* and *Romeo and Juliet* to *Twelfth Night, Troilus and Cressida* and *Hamlet,* carrying the revolution begun

The King's Servant

Middle Temple Hall, where *Twelfth Night* was performed, 2 Feb. 1602

The first Shakespeare anecdote, as told by John Manningham of the Middle Temple, 1602

by the University Wits to heights undreamed of by the envious Greene. Moreover, his achievement and example had produced a school of dramatists the like of which had never been seen before, and has never been seen since, in England or in any other country. Yet success had not spoiled him; he was still as modest and civil as Chettle had found him ten years before, and still as popular with 'divers of worship' at the Inns of Court, where his plays were performed and he was affectionately known as William the Conqueror.

Despite its promise the Jacobean age began inauspiciously. Plague came in with James, the theatres were closed, and 30,000 people died in London before they were reopened in the following spring. It was the worst visitation of Shakespeare's lifetime. The King's Men went on tour, performing *Hamlet* both at Oxford and Cambridge, with the result that one of their hirelings, probably he who played Marcellus, memorised and wrote a version for a publisher. So a sixth 'bad' quarto, the most famous of all, appeared in London at the height of the plague. Shakespeare himself probably retired to New Place to revise the recalcitrant *All's Well,* which had as yet not ended well, and to write *Measure for Measure,* a sombre and experimental comedy whose title reveals a more serious intent than its light-hearted predecessors, *Much Ado about Nothing, As You Like It, What You Will.* By November he had rejoined his company and was rehearsing for the Revels at Mortlake, up the river from London, when they received an order to to go to Wilton, the Earl of Pembroke's house near Salisbury. The Court was there, and on December 2nd Shakespeare and his fellows gave their first performance before the King, the play being, apparently, *As You Like It.* Soon afterwards James left Wilton for Hampton Court, where his first Christmas Revels were held. The King's gave seven plays, one of which was *A Midsummer Night's Dream,* and another Jonson's unsuccessful tragedy *Sejanus,* in which Shakespeare took part. It is the last record of his acting, and it may be that from now on he was free to devote all his time to writing and the

Wilton House. 'We have the man Shakespeare with us'— to present *As You Like It* before King James, 2 Dec. 1603

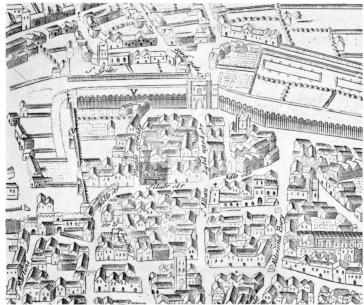

Christopher Mountjoy's house,
at the corner of Mugle Street and Silver Street
near Cripplegate,
where Shakespeare was lodging in 1604

producing of plays. In *Hamlet* we catch a glimpse of him coaching his fellows: 'Speak the speech, I pray you, as I pronounced it to you, trippingly on the tongue . . . Suit the action to the word, the word to the action, with this special observance, that you o'erstep not the modesty of nature.' The medieval tradition of ranting, of tearing a passion to tatters, died hard, but Shakespeare would have none of it in his company. His withdrawal from acting made room for new men, and the fellowship was increased from nine to twelve sharers.

By the end of February the plague was almost over, and Shakespeare found new London lodgings near Cripplegate, at the corner of Monkwell (Mugle) Street and Silver Street, in the house of Christopher Mountjoy, a maker of tires, the costly and elaborate headdresses worn by ladies. Here he got involved in a family affair. Mountjoy had a daughter Mary, whom he wished to see married to his apprentice Stephen Belott, and Shakespeare good-naturedly agreed to further the romance. He brought to bear on Belott what must have been his very considerable powers of persuasion, pointing out that there would be an enviable marriage portion with Mary, with hints perhaps of more to follow on her father's death. Stephen's diffidence was overcome. Shakespeare betrothed them by making them take each other's hand, and they were married in November. It was not the last that he was to hear of the matter.

The Great Tragedies It was probably at the Mountjoys' that he began to write *Othello*. The dramatic prose of his histories and comedies had taught him to write dramatic

The Somerset House Conference, 1604, when Shakespeare was on duty as a Groom of the Chamber

poetry, verse creative of character, perfected in *Hamlet* and *Measure for Measure*. Now, at the height of his powers, he applied this noble medium to the noblest of dramatic forms, tragedy. There is no need to assume that he was now, and for the next few years, himself in tragic mood; a man does not necessarily take to tragic themes because he is unhappy—Falstaff had been Shakespeare's reply to the disaster of Hamnet's death—but a great poet and dramatist will turn to tragedy if he wishes to create the highest form of art, and *Othello* is only the first of the series of tremendous tragedies that culminated in *Antony and Cleopatra* four years later. Even for Burbage, playing the tragic heroes at the Globe, the strain must have been considerable, but for Shakespeare it must have been almost unbearable, as month after month he lived the parts and suffered with the characters he was creating—for this complete self-identification is one of the main secrets of his art—suffered the jealousy of Othello, the madness of Timon and Lear, the remorse of Macbeth, the insane pride of Coriolanus and the despair of Antony.

In March the King was able to make his long delayed state progress through the City, and Shakespeare as a Groom of the Chamber was given his scarlet livery for the occasion. He was soon called upon to wear it again in an official capacity. In August Cecil negotiated peace with Spain, and the King's Men were appointed to attend the Spanish Ambassador Extraordinary at Somerset House. It was peace with honour, the most successful political event of the

'Shaxberd' at Whitehall. The Revels Account for 1604/5

reign. The twenty years' war with Spain was over. And yet those twenty anxious years had seen, had stimulated, the great Elizabethan literary renaissance.

No wonder the Revels that Christmas were joyful and prolonged, from the beginning of November to the end of February. Fortunately the accounts of the Master of the Revels for this season of 1604/5 have been preserved. Of the eleven plays presented by the King's Men at least seven were Shakespeare's: *Othello, The Merry Wives of Windsor, Measure for Measure, The Comedy of Errors, Love's Labour's Lost, Henry V* and *The Merchant of Venice,* which was given twice. They also gave two performances of Jonson's comedies.

Jonson claimed Scottish descent and was not slow to exploit this fortunate ancestry, in conjunction with the Queen's passion for extravagant display. In Elizabeth's reign the masque had been little more than a modest form of charade involving dressing up and dancing, but under Jonson it developed into an elaborate pageantry set off by the most spectacular scenic effects. The actors were the Queen herself and the great ones of the Court, the ladies wearing jewellery worth more than a monarch's revenue. To design the costumes and the scenery

Jonson secured the help of the rising young architect, Inigo Jones, and the long collaboration of these two great men began on Twelfth Night, 1605, with the *Masque of Blackness,* in which the Queen and her ladies appeared as blackamoors. During the next few years Jonson was establishing his position at Court by writing and rehearsing these ephemeral and lovely trifles, while Shakespeare was engaged with his great tragedies. *Timon of Athens* and the greater part of *King Lear* were probably written in 1605.

If Shakespeare was in Stratford as early as April he would certainly attend the wedding of Robert Harvard of Southwark and Katherine Rogers, the daughter of his neighbour Thomas Rogers, and even if he were not there would soon meet them at their home on Bankside, where their famous son, John Harvard, was born two years later. In the following month he lost an old friend, Augustine Phillips, one of the original members of the Chamberlain's company. The most loyal of men, he left legacies to most of his fellows, including 'a thirty shillings peece in gould' to Shakespeare. He seems to have been in Stratford by July, when he invested £440, a very large sum, in the tithes of the fields adjoining his estate to the north of the town. There he would meet his new neighbour at Clopton House, the wealthy young Catholic, Ambrose Rookwood. It is just possible that he was still at New Place at the beginning of November, for plague had returned to London and the theatres were closed. If so, he would see something of the excitement on the 6th. The

A design by Inigo Jones for the *Masque of Blackness*

Clopton House, Stratford,
a base for the Gunpowder Plot

Gunpowder Plot had miscarried, Guy Fawkes had been arrested, and the other conspirators had fled to their strongholds in the Midlands, one of which was Clopton House. It was raided by the borough constables, but Rookwood had flown. Two days later he was captured, and was executed with Fawkes in front of the Parliament House which they had attempted to blow up.

The King's Men gave ten plays that Christmas, and we can imagine James, after the performance of one of Shakespeare's histories, buttonholing the author and suggesting that as he had written so many plays about English history he might like to try his hand at a Scottish theme. Perhaps one of his ancestors. . . . He may not have added that he was expecting a visit from his brother-in-law, Christian IV of Denmark, in the summer. Plays by his own company would be an essential part of the entertainment, and Christian would certainly expect to see a performance of *The Prince of Denmark*. Apart from being the most appropriate of plays, *Hamlet* was also the most famous; quoted everywhere in London, it had been exported to Germany, and was even acted on the high seas. Shakespeare took the hint and, having finished *King Lear* (it was acted at Court in December), turned up the Scottish history in Holinshed's *Chronicles*,

was right displeasant to him and his people, as shoulde appeare in that it was a custome many yeares after, that no Knightes were made in Norway, excepte they were firste sworne to reuenge the slaughter of theyr countreymen and frendes thus slayne in Scotland.

The othe that knights tooke in Norway, to reuenge the death of theyr frendes.

The Scottes hauing wonne so notable a bictory, after they had gathered and diuided the spoyle of the fielde, caused solemne processions to be made in all places of the realme, and thankes to be giuen to almightie God, that had sent them so fayre a day ouer their enimies.

Solemne processions for victory gotte.

But whylest the people were thus at theyr processions, worde was brought that a newe fleete of Danes was arriued at Kingcorne, sent thyther by Canute king of England in reuenge of his brothers Suenoes ouerthrow.

A power of Danes arriue at Kyncorne out of Englāil.

To resist these enimies, whiche were already landed, and busie in spoiling the countrey, Makbeth and Banquho were sente with the kings authoritie, who hauing with them a conuenient power, encountred the enimies, slewe parte of them, and chased the other to their shippes. They that escaped and got once to theyr shippes, obtayned of Makbeth for a great summe of golde, that suche of theyr freendes as were slaine at this last bickering might be buried in Saint Colmes Inche. In memorie whereof, many olde Sepultures are yet in the sayde Inche, there to be seene grauen with the armes of the Danes, as

The Danes vanquished by Makbeth and Banquho.

Danes buried in S. Colmes Inche.

the maner of burying noble men still is, and heretofore hath bene bsed.

A peace was also concluded at the same time betwirte the Danes and Scottishmen, ratified as some haue wryten in this wise. That from thence foorth the Danes shoulde neuer come into Scotlande to make any warres agaynst the Scottes by any maner of meanes.

A peace concluded betwixt Scottes and Danes.

And these were the warres that Duncane had with forrayne enimics in the seuenth yeare of his reygne.

Shortly after happened a straunge and bncouth wonder, whiche afterwarde was the cause of muche trouble in the realme of Scotlande as ye shall after heare. It fortuned as Makbeth & Banquho iourneyed towarde Fores, where the king as then lay, they went sporting by the way together without other companie, saue only theselues, passing through the woodes and fieldes, when sodenly in the middes of a lavide, there met them.iij. women in straunge & ferly apparell, resembling creatures of an elder worlde, whom when they attentiuely behelde, wondering much at the sight. The first of them spake & sayde: Ill hayle Makbeth Thane of Glammis (for he had lately entred into that dignitie and office by the death of his father Synel.) The.ij.of them said: Hayle Makbeth Thane of Cawder: but the third sayde: Ill Hayle Makbeth that hereafter shall be king of Scotland.

The prophesie of three women supposing to be the weird sisters or feiries.

Then Banquho, what maner of women (saith he) are you, that seeme so litle fauourable bnto me, where as to my fellow here, besides highe offices, yee assigne also the kingdome, appointyng foorth nothing for me at all? Yes sayth the firste of them, wee promise greater benefites bnto thee, than bnto him, for he shall reygne in in deede, but with an bnluckie ende: neyther shall he leaue any issue behinde him to succeede

in his place, where contrariy thou in deede shalt not reygne at all, but of thee those shall be borne whiche shall gouerne the Scottishe kingdome by long order of continuall discent. Herewith the foresayde women banished immediatly out of theyr sight . This was reputed at the first but some bayne fantasticall illusion by Makbeth and Banquho , in so muche that Banquho woulde call Makbeth in ieste kyng of

A thing to wonder at.

Q.ij.   Scot-

found the story of Macbeth, and began to write. Unfortunately Christian was preceded by plague, and the festivities had to be held outside the capital, so that it was at Greenwich that the King's Men presented before the royal rivals two plays, one of which must have been *Hamlet*. A few days later at Hampton Court, to the great satisfaction of James, *Hamlet* was capped by *Macbeth*.

Holinshed's *Chronicles*, uninspired though they were, had served Shakespeare well, but for his last two tragedies he turned to the noble prose of Sir Thomas North's translation of Plutarch, *The Lives of the Noble Grecians and Romans*. He may have finished *Coriolanus* and been already engaged on *Antony and Cleopatra* when, in June, 1607, his elder daughter Susanna, now a woman of twenty-four, married Dr. John Hall. The young physician was making a great reputation for himself, not only in Stratford, but throughout the county and even beyond. Some years later he began to compile a case-book, 'Observations' so well esteemed that they were translated from the original Latin and published twenty years after his death. By 1607 he could afford to live spaciously, so he bought a half-timbered house near the church, enlarged it to include an impressive consulting-room and dispensary, and there installed himself with his bride.

New Place would now have only two occupants for the greater part of the year, Anne and Judith, and Shakespeare looked round for companions for his wife and younger daughter. The new town clerk, Thomas Greene, was his distant cousin, married, with two small children, just the sort of family to enliven the big house, and before returning to London Shakespeare arranged that they should move into New Place, on the understanding that they would have to leave when he retired.

He was in no hurry to return, for plague had again closed the theatres, and his company was on tour. But he was back by November, and at Whitehall on December 28th for the presentation of a play. This may have been the day on which his young brother Edmund died, for he was buried in the church of St. Saviour's, only a few yards from the Globe, on the morning of the 31st. We do not know what company of players he had joined; perhaps he was a hireling with the King's, waiting for a vacancy as sharer in the fellowship, but we may be sure that it was his brother who paid for the expensive funeral, with the solemn tolling of the great bell.

A few months later Shakespeare lost his mother. She may have gone to live at New Place after the death of her husband, but more probably stayed in Henley Street with Joan and her two little grandsons. The house now belonged to Shakespeare, who let it to his sister and brother-in-law at a nominal rent, and perhaps his bachelor brothers moved into the eastern half where they still carried on their father's business. But more important to Shakespeare than the loss of his mother was the coming of a grandchild. In the previous February

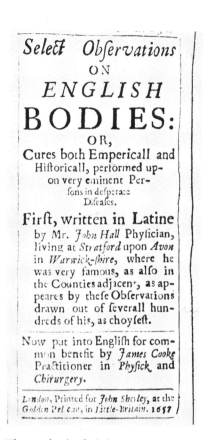

The case-book of Shakespeare's son-in-law   Hall's Croft, the home of Shakespeare's daughter, Susanna

Susanna had given birth to a daughter.

The birth of Elizabeth Hall in 1608 coincided with important developments in the affairs of the King's Men. The Children of the Revels had got into difficulties, and in August their manager surrendered the Blackfriars theatre to its owners, the Burbage brothers, who formed a syndicate of seven house-keepers, including Shakespeare, Heminge and Condell. The company now had another playhouse on the other side of the river as their winter quarters, an acquisition of immense significance. They were the first company of adult actors to perform regularly in a small roofed theatre, and obviously this involved a modification not only in their style of acting but in their type of play as well. The Globe was an open theatre, cold and draughty in winter, with room for an audience of two or three thousand, half of whom stood in the yard. The Black-friars was snug and intimate, and held only two or three hundred, all of whom were seated. Moreover, the audience at the Globe was a cross-section of society,

Two new dramatists engaged by the King's Men to write for their Blackfriars theatre: John Fletcher, Francis Beaumont

from courtier to carter, but only the wealthier and more educated classes could afford seats at Blackfriars. Something on a smaller scale than Shakespeare's titanic tragedies was called for, and the King's Men engaged two young dramatists who had already written for the boys at Blackfriars. So began the famous collaboration of Beaumont and Fletcher and their series of sweet, courtly, sentimental romances bearing little or no resemblance to real life. It was the beginning of the degeneration of the virile Elizabethan drama nurtured in the open theatres.

Shakespeare, too, began to write for the Blackfriars stage. Having brought his tragic art to perfection in *Antony and Cleopatra*, he turned again to romance, though more grave and lyrical in treatment than his middle comedies, and by November had written *Pericles,* the story of the sea-born Marina. There can be little doubt that the inspiration was his granddaughter, an inspiration carried over into his last three plays, in which the essential theme is the fortunes of his young heroines, Imogen, Perdita and Miranda. After the strain of four years of tragedy the relief must have been sweet indeed.

'In the Winters Talle at the glob
1611 the 15 of Maye.'
Simon Forman describes a performance

'His sugred Sonnets among his priuate friends'

SHAKE-SPEARES

SONNETS.

Neuer before Imprinted.

AT LONDON
By *G. Eld* for *T. T.* and are
to be folde by *Iohn Wright,* dwelling
at Chriſt Church gate.
1609.

Perhaps the publication of *King Lear* in 1608, followed by *Pericles* and *Troilus and Cressida* in 1609, had something to do with raising money for the Blackfriars venture, though the first two are sufficiently poor texts to warrant suspicion of piracy. The *Sonnets*, too, which at last appeared in 1609, may have been issued without Shakespeare's permission. These were the last of his works to be published in his lifetime, though the quartos that had already been printed continued to go through new editions, and his popularity is further attested by the plays issued with his name by stationers more enterprising than honest. For example, *A Yorkshire Tragedy,* a King's play it is true, was published in 1608 as 'written by W. Shakspeare'.

Probably Shakespeare spent much of 1609 at New Place, as plague closed the theatres for most of the year. This annual recurrence of plague in London inevitably made him think of retirement to Stratford, but he decided to wait another year, and in September Thomas Greene made a note that he could 'stay another yere at newe place'. But 1610 was little better; by the end of June plague deaths were mounting, the theatres were closed again, the players once

The Last Years

'A play Called the Tempest.' The Revels Account for 1611‑12

more took to the road, and Shakespeare, now aged forty‑six, gave up his London lodgings and retired to Stratford, where he finished *The Winter's Tale*.

Ironically enough, plague lifted soon after his move and did not affect London again while he lived, so that for the next year or two he probably spent as much time as ever with his company. He may have been with them when they crossed the river from Blackfriars to the Globe in April, and presented *Macbeth, The Winter's Tale* and *Cymbeline*. These were all seen by the physician and astrologer Simon Forman, who made notes on them in his *Booke of Plaies*. The pity is that they are merely summaries of the plots, the doctor in *Macbeth* being, apparently, his favourite character. If only he had written a description of the productions and of how Burbage played Macbeth and Leontes he could so easily have won the fame for which he thirsted, without the desperate recourse to suicide a few weeks later, on the day that he had predicted for his death.

In the previous autumn Shakespeare had read the accounts of the wreck of Sir George Somers on the Bermudas, and probably spoken to some of the survivors. The story moved him strangely, for storms and wrecks were much in his mind at this time, and in the course of 1611 he wrote his last and loveliest

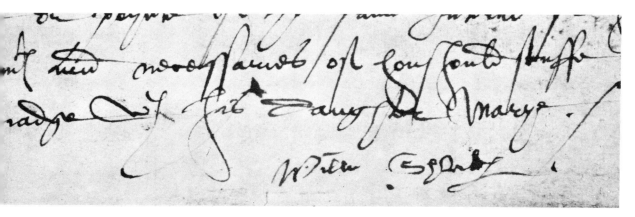

And more he cannot depose.' Shakespeare signs his deposition in the case of *Belott v. Mountjoy*, 11 May 1612

play, *The Tempest*. There can be little doubt that he was at Whitehall for its production on November 1st, when the Revels began. It was followed by *The Winter's Tale*, and altogether the King's Men gave twenty-two plays that season, which was prolonged to the end of April.

He stayed in London a little longer. There was no alternative, for he had been called as witness in a case brought by Stephen Belott against his father-in-law, who had failed to make over the dowry promised with his daughter. On May 11th, 1612, 'William Shakespeare of Stratford vpon Aven, gentleman, of the age of xlviij yeres or thereaboutes' was questioned by a lawyer. It is strange to hear the echo of his voice. Yes, he had known the Mountjoys for some ten years, and had helped to persuade Stephen, 'a very good and industrious servant', to marry Mary. It was true that Mountjoy had promised a marriage portion, but how much it was he had quite forgotten, and he remembered nothing at all about a promised legacy. He was not very helpful, but there was no reason why he should remember such details after eight years, and having signed his deposition he made for Stratford. He had work to do.

His retirement, or semi-retirement, would have been disastrous to the King's Men if Beaumont and Fletcher had not been there to supply them with new plays, rapidly becoming almost as popular as his own. When, therefore, Beaumont married an heiress and withdrew from the theatre they were in great distress. Fletcher needed the stimulus of a collaborator, and until he found another among the younger men they implored Shakespeare to write with him. It would not be very arduous work; if he would set the play going by introducing the main themes and characters Fletcher would see to the rest. Shakespeare readily agreed and began to sketch out *Cardenio*, a play that has been lost, though it was produced at the Revels of 1612-13. These were the most brilliant of the reign, in celebration of the marriage of James's daughter Elizabeth to

Princess Elizabeth and the Elector Palatine,
whose betrothal was celebrated by a performance of *The Tempest*

Queen Anne and Henry, Prince of Wales,
who died during his sister's
wedding festivities

the Elector Palatine, and Shakespeare must have been there to supervise the production of *The Tempest, Julius Caesar, Much Ado, Othello, The Winter's Tale,* and the two parts of *Henry IV. The Tempest* was almost certainly given on the eve of the betrothal, and we may, perhaps, imagine Shakespeare playing his last part that night as Prospero, blessing the young couple—for they were only children—and wishing them the happiness that was, alas, so soon to elude them.

The festivities were marred by the sudden death of Henry, Prince of Wales, a young man of great promise, but after a pause they were resumed. In March, before their conclusion, Shakespeare bought the gatehouse of the Blackfriars priory, near the theatre, raising part of the money by a mortgage, a transaction in which he was helped by his friends John Heminge and William Johnson, landlord of the Mermaid Tavern. It was at the Mermaid, near St. Paul's, that Shakespeare, Jonson, Fletcher, Donne and other leading wits used to forgather and dine on the first Friday of the month, when words were nimble and full of subtle flame. A few days later he was associated with another old friend, Dick

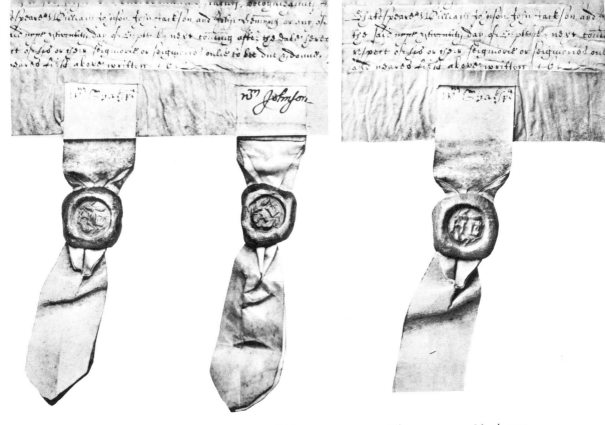

Shakespeare buys a London house. He and his trustee, the landlord of the Mermaid, sign the conveyance, 10 March 1613

The mortgage, 11 March 1613, with Shakespeare's signature

Burbage, in a very different matter. This was the designing and making for the Duke of Rutland of an 'impresa', a device painted on a pasteboard shield carried by his squire before a tilt. Burbage, we know, was an amateur painter, and it looks as though Shakespeare may have been one too.

In the middle of April the Elector and Elizabeth set out for Germany, and the Court left London. But Shakespeare probably lingered. Fletcher had recently finished the history of *Henry VIII* which he had half written for him, and it was soon to be produced at the Globe. Perhaps, however, he was already back in Stratford when, on that fatal Tuesday, June 29th, the Globe was burned to the ground during a performance of the play. The wadding from a gun fired on the entry of King Henry set fire to the thatch, and within an hour the galleries had crashed into the yard, and the heavens and hell were consumed together among the flaming timbers. The audience escaped by a miracle, 'only one man had his breeches set on fire, that would perhaps have broiled him, if he had not by the benefit of a provident wit put it out with bottle ale'. 'Nothing',

John Shakespeare's workshop converted into an inn

we are told, 'did perish but wood and straw and a few forsaken cloaks'. If the King's Men kept their stock of plays in the Globe, somehow they were saved, and with them the priceless manuscript plays of Shakespeare. The house-keepers had to shoulder the cost of rebuilding, and it may be that Shakespeare relinquished his share to a more active member of the company.

From now on he spent most of his time in Stratford. Gilbert and Richard had both died in the last year. Their father's old workshop was let and con-verted into an inn, known as the Swan and Maidenhead, and Joan and her family—there were now three boys—were left in sole possession of the Henley Street house. The pity was that there were no small boys in the Hall house, no grandsons. Elizabeth was the only child of Susanna, whom, incidentally, Shakespeare had to help to clear of an irresponsible and slanderous charge soon after his return from London. Some of his old friends, Richard Quiney among them, had gone, but others remained. There were, for example, Henry Walker, of whose young son he was godfather, his neighbours Hamnet and Judith Sadler, godparents of his own children, and next door but one to New Place was Julyne Shaw. The brothers John and Anthony Nash lived in Old Strat-ford, and at Clifford Chambers over the river was Sir Henry Rainsford with whom Michael Drayton sometimes stayed. Thomas Russell lived a little further afield in the manor house at Aldminster. Then there was the wealthy

John Combe, 'vpon whose name Shakespeere did merrily fann vp some witty and facetious verses'

bachelor and money-lender, John Combe. He died in July, 1614, on the day after the third great fire to ravage the town, and was buried by the altar in the parish church. He left £5 to Shakespeare, who probably found the sculptor to make his tomb and effigy, Gerard Johnson, the Bankside mason.

At this time Shakespeare was involved in a scheme to enclose the open fields bordering his estate. Although he was not one of the promoters, as a tithe-owner he would be affected, probably favourably. His attitude, however, is uncertain, and the main interest of the controversy lies in the notes made by Thomas Greene, who, as town clerk, was employed by the Corporation to prevent the enclosure. Shakespeare may have gone up to London in the spring for the opening of the new Globe theatre, rebuilt 'in far finer manner than before', with a tiled roof to the galleries instead of thatch, for he would want to see what Fletcher had made of his contribution to *The Two Noble Kinsmen*—not very much as it happened. He was certainly there in November with John Hall, when Greene, who was already up on enclosure business, called 'to see him howe he did' and to ask how things were going in Stratford. His 'Cosen

The painted room in the Crown Tavern, Oxford, where Shakespeare is said
to have lodged on his journeys between London and Stratford.
It was kept by John Davenant, and tradition has it that Shakespeare
was godfather of his son, William

Thomas Greene makes his last note on 'my Cosen Shakspeare'

The second Globe theatre and Beargarden. (The names are interchanged.) The Blackfriars theatre
is probably the long building above and to the right of the flag

Shakspeare' assured him that although 'they meane in Aprill to servey the
Land . . . there will be nothyng done at all'. He was right, though the controversy dragged on, and nearly a year later, in September, 1615, Greene inserted
a note in his memoranda: 'W Shakspeares tellyng J Greene [Thomas's
brother] that I was not able to beare the encloseinge of Welcombe'. It is the
last record we have of Shakespeare before he made his will a few months later.

When he was in London at the end of 1614 he would meet Ben Jonson and
learn of his project to publish a collected edition of his 'Works'. No doubt this
set him thinking along the same lines, for, now that Fletcher had found new
collaborators and the King's Men were no longer in urgent need of his help,
how could he better employ his longed-for leisure than in preparing his own
works for a similar collected edition? After all, he had been abominably careless
about the publication of his plays. Half of them, indeed, had never been published, and some of these were scarcely in a state for the press; then, the printed
texts of many of the remainder were most inaccurate, and four of the corrupt
pirated quartos had never been replaced by a genuine version. There was plenty
of work for the next year or two, and we may imagine him in 1615 revising

and rewriting some of his manuscript plays, the still recalcitrant *All's Well that Ends Well,* for example, in his study at New Place.

By the beginning of 1616 preparations were afoot for the marriage of Judith and Thomas Quiney, son of his old friend Richard, and in January, being then 'in perfect health', he got Francis Collins, a Warwick solicitor, to draw up a will providing for both his daughters. A few weeks after the wedding, which was on February 10th, he was taken seriously ill. According to an old tradition, 'Shakespear, Drayton and Ben Jhonson had a merry meeting, and it seems drank too hard, for Shakespear died of a feavour there contracted'. It is possible. Drayton might have been at Clifford Chambers early in the year, though Jonson was probably much too busy with masques and revels at Whitehall. Perhaps the merry meeting, if there really was one, took place in London to celebrate the publication of Jonson's folio edition of his *Works.* If Shakespeare was taken ill there, he might have been a very sick man by the time he reached Stratford after riding ninety miles in cold March weather. But whatever happened, he sent for Collins again, and, after revising his will, signed it on March 25th. Anne was provided for by her widow's dower, and his only mention of her is the famous 'vnto my wief my second best bed'. It was the bed on which he was dying. To Judith he left a substantial marriage portion; to Joan £20, all his 'wearing Apparrell'—it would come in useful for her sons— and the Henley Street house for life. With a few exceptions all the rest of his estate was to go to Susanna and her heirs male, if any. The death of Hamnet had ruined his plan of founding a family, but Susanna's sons would at least be lineal descendants. It was a vain hope. Elizabeth was Susanna's only child, and Elizabeth, though twice married, had no children at all. Judith's three sons all died young, and only the collateral line of Joan and the Harts survived. Among the minor legatees were his 'ffellowes John Hemynge Richard Burbage & Henry Cundell', to whom he left 26s. 8d. 'a peece to buy them Ringes'. They were the sole survivors of the original Chamberlain's fellowship formed more than twenty years ago.

His brother-in-law was dying in Henley Street, and on April 17th 'Will. Hartt, hatter' was buried. Presumably Dr. Hall attended them both. He was to cure Michael Drayton, 'an excellent poet', of a fever, but an even more excellent poet he was unable to save. Shakespeare died a week after the funeral of Joan's husband, possibly on his fifty-second birthday. On April 25th he was taken from New Place, past the Gild Chapel and Grammar School, down the road to the church along which he had been carried to his christening exactly fifty-two years before, and buried in front of the altar. Gerard Johnson was commissioned to make the monument that was set up on the wall overlooking his grave.

'By me William Shakspeare.' The last of the three pages of his will ▶

Males of the bodie of the said ffourth sonne lawfull yssueinge for lyfe and as it is before Lymitted to be remaine to the first second and third sonns of her bodie and theire heires males lawfull and for lack of such issue the said things to be remaine to my said Moore Hall and the heires males of her bodie lawfull and for defaulte of such issue to my daughter Judith and the heires males of her bodie lawfully issueinge And for want of such issue to the right heires of me the said William Earthbrowe for ever . . . . . . and equallye to my said daughter Judith my . . . . . . And all the rest of my goods chattells . . . . plate jewells and househould stuffe whatsoever after my dettes and Legacies paied and my funerall expences discharged I geve devise and bequeath to my sonne in Lawe John Hall gent and my daughter Susanna his wife whom I ordaine and make executors of this my said Last will and testam't And I doe intreat and Appoint Thomas . . . . and . . . . gent to be assistants herof And I doe revoke all former wills and publishe this to be my Last will and testam't . . . . . . in witnes Wherof . . . . . . I have herevnto put my hand the daie and yeare first above written.

witnes to the publishing
hereof   ffr: Collyns
Johnn Shawe
Jo: Robinson
Samuel Sadler
Robert Wigfield

By me William Shakspeare

Probatum coram magro. Will'mo . . .
Legum doctore Commiss . . . .
mens . . . Anno d'ni 1616 . . . . .
Johannis Hall . . . .
second . . . . iurat . . . .
. . . . Hall ad . . . . ind
. . . .

'Will Shakspere gent'.
The entry of his burial
in Stratford Parish Register

Shakespeare's monument and grave within the sanctuary of Holy Trinity Church, Stratford ▶

What then? What remained? Why all this pother about a provincial boy who made a fortune out of the theatre? The question was answered seven years later when Heminge and Condell completed the work that Shakespeare had entrusted to them, the editing of his plays and their publication in a single volume. Had it not been for their devotion half of them, including *Twelfth Night* and *Macbeth, Antony and Cleopatra* and *The Tempest,* might have perished unpublished, and of *Henry V* and three others we should have only the mutilated versions of the 'bad' quartos. But Shakespeare's friends brought out the precious manuscripts from the King's Men's store, some his originals, others fair copies, and from these the yet unpublished plays were printed, as well as those 'maimed and deformed by the frauds and stealthes of iniurious impostors'. The remainder were set up from their quartos, corrected by reference to the manuscripts. This, then, remained: the thirty-six plays of the Folio, perhaps the greatest single creative achievement of man. It is a large claim.

Yet among the poets of the world there are only one or two with any claim to be of Shakespeare's stature. Will you have pure lyric? There are the songs, from 'Who is Silvia' in *The Two Gentlemen of Verona* to 'Full fathom five' in *The Tempest.* Or sonnets? There are a hundred and fifty, from which one may choose at random:

> *Shall I compare thee to a summer's day?*
> *Thou art more lovely and more temperate:*
> *Rough winds do shake the darling buds of May,*
> *And summer's lease hath all too short a date.*

or,

> *When lofty trees I see barren of leaves,*
> *Which erst from heat did canopy the herd,*
> *And summer's green all girded up in sheaves,*
> *Born on the bier with white and bristly beard,*
> *Then of thy beauty do I question make,*
> *That thou among the wastes of time must go.*

The same princely poetry is the stuff of the early lyrical plays:

> *It was the lark, the herald of the morn,*
> *No nightingale: look, love, what envious streaks*
> *Do lace the severing clouds in yonder east:*
> *Night's candles are burned out, and jocund day*
> *Stands tiptoe on the misty mountain top.*

The monument overlooking the grave ▶

And to a similar, though more intricate and golden lyricism Shakespeare returned in his last romances:

> *Daffodils,*
> *That come before the swallow dares, and take*
> *The winds of March with beauty; violets dim,*
> *But sweeter than the lids of Juno's eyes*
> *Or Cytherea's breath.*

Then, Shakespeare was doubly a maker, a creator not only of poetry but of people, and here no other poet approaches him. No other writer has ever created a comparable company of men and women, humble and exalted, grave and gay, comic and tragic, noble and ignoble: Launce, Bottom, Dogberry, Pistol, Autolycus, Juliet's nurse, Mistress Quickly; Falstaff, Touchstone, Jaques, Feste, Malvolio, Parolles, Benedick; Julia, Beatrice, Rosalind, Viola, Helena, Marina, Imogen, Perdita, Miranda; Richard II, Richard III, King John, Henry V, Hotspur, Brutus, Hamlet, Othello, Iago, Lear, Macbeth; Juliet, Desdemona, Cordelia, Volumnia, Lady Macbeth, Cleopatra—the list might be almost indefinitely extended. The wonder is that they are nothing but words, and the final wonder is the words themselves, the poetry in which they talk themselves alive. For they *are* the poetry. This *is* Juliet:

> *Come, gentle night, come, loving, black-brow'd night,*
> *Give me my Romeo; and, when he shall die,*
> *Take him and cut him out in little stars,*
> *And he will make the face of heaven so fine,*
> *That all the world will be in love with night.*

This Hamlet:

> *O good Horatio, what a wounded name,*
> *Things standing thus unknown, shall live behind me!*
> *If thou didst ever hold me in thy heart,*
> *Absent thee from felicity a while,*
> *And in this harsh world draw thy breath in pain,*
> *To tell my story.*

This Cleopatra:

>   *O, see, my women,*
> *The crown o' the earth doth melt. My lord!*
> *O, wither'd is the garland of the war,*
> *The soldier's pole is fall'n: young boys and girls*
> *Are level now with men; the odds is gone,*
> *And there is nothing left remarkable*
> *Beneath the visiting moon.*

Title page of the First Folio ▶

Mr. WILLIAM
SHAKESPEARES

COMEDIES,
HISTORIES, &
TRAGEDIES.

Published according to the True Originall Copies.

Martin Droeshout sculpsit London.

LONDON
Printed by Isaac Iaggard, and Ed. Blount. 1623.

But this, we feel, is Shakespeare, one of the rare glimpses we catch of him in his plays:

> Our revels now are ended. These our actors,
> As I foretold you, were all spirits, and
> Are melted into air, into thin air:
> And, like the baseless fabric of this vision,
> The cloud-capp'd towers, the gorgeous palaces,
> The solemn temples, the great globe itself,
> Yea, all which it inherit shall dissolve,
> And, like this insubstantial pageant faded,
> Leave not a rack behind. We are such stuff
> As dreams are made on; and our little life
> Is rounded with a sleep.

Although Shakespeare is so elusive, because so protean, ever changing from one character to another, his spirit permeates the plays, and we read them not only for the poetry and the people we meet there, but also for the man he was. That is what, above all, makes them so consolatory. We read them for his genial wisdom, his flooding noonday illumination of life, his gaiety and wit, his essential sanity: because he was the ideally normal man, whose far-ranging faculties were all perfectly attuned and harmonised. We read Shakespeare because he is the man whom we should all like to have for friend.

———————————————>∞c<———————————————

Here follow five pages from the First Folio ▶

To the great Variety of Readers.

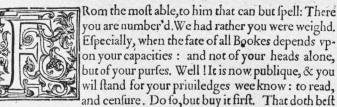

Rom the most able, to him that can but spell: There you are number'd. We had rather you were weighd. Especially, when the fate of all Bookes depends vpon your capacities : and not of your heads alone, but of your purses. Well ! It is now publique, & you wil stand for your priuiledges wee know : to read, and censure. Do so, but buy it first. That doth best commend a Booke, the Stationer saies. Then, how odde soeuer your braines be, or your wisedomes, make your licence the same, and spare not. Iudge your sixe-pen'orth, your shillings worth, your fiue shillings worth at a time, or higher, so you rise to the iust rates, and welcome. But, what euer you do, Buy. Censure will not driue a Trade, or make the Iacke go. And though you be a Magistrate of wit, and sit on the Stage at *Black-Friers*, or the *Cock-pit*, to arraigne Playes dailie, know, these Playes haue had their triall alreadie, and stood out all Appeales ; and do now come forth quitted rather by a Decree of Court, then any purchas'd Letters of commendation.

It had bene a thing, we confesse, worthie to haue bene wished, that the Author himselfe had liu'd to haue set forth, and ouerseen his owne writings ; But since it hath bin ordain'd otherwise, and he by death departed from that right, we pray you do not envie his Friends, the office of their care, and paine, to haue collected & publish'd them; and so to haue publish'd them, as where (before) you were abus'd with diuerse stolne, and surreptitious copies, maimed, and deformed by the frauds and stealthes of iniurious impostors, that expos'd them : euen those, are now offer'd to your view cur'd, and perfect of their limbes; and all the rest, absolute in their numbers, as he conceiued thē. Who, as he was a happie imitator of Nature, was a most gentle expresser of it. His mind and hand went together : And what he thought, he vttered with that easinesse, that wee haue scarse receiued from him a blot in his papers. But it is not our prouince, who onely gather his works, and giue them you, to praise him. It is yours that reade him. And there we hope, to your diuers capacities, you will finde enough, both to draw, and hold you : for his wit can no more lie hid, then it could be lost. Reade him, therefore ; and againe, and againe : And if then you doe not like him, surely you are in some manifest danger, not to vnderstand him. And so we leaue you to other of his Friends, whom if you need, can bee your guides : if you neede them not, you can leade your selues, and others. And such Readers we wish him.

A 3

Iohn Heminge.
Henrie Condell.

William Sly,
one of the original members of Shakespeare's company
John Lowin,
who played Falstaff, and in the part of Henry VIII
'had his instructions from Mr. Shakespear himself'
Nathan Field,
playwright as well as player,
who replaced Shakespeare in the King's Company

The Workes of William Shakespeare,
containing all his Comedies, Histories, and
Tragedies: Truely set forth, according to their first
ORIGINALL.

The Names of the Principall Actors
in all these Playes.

William Shakespeare.

Richard Burbadge.

John Hemmings.

Augustine Phillips.

William Kempt.

Thomas Poope.

George Bryan.

Henry Condell.

William Slye.

Richard Cowly.

John Lowine.

Samuell Crosse.

Alexander Cooke.

Samuel Gilburne.

Robert Armin.

William Ostler.

Nathan Field.

John Underwood.

Nicholas Tooley.

William Ecclestone.

Joseph Taylor.

Robert Benfield.

Robert Goughe.

Richard Robinson.

Iohn Shancke.

Iohn Rice.

A CATALOGVE

of the feuerall Comedies, Histories, and Tragedies contained in this Volume.

THE TEMPEST.

Actus primus, Scena prima.

A tempestuous noise of Thunder and Lightning heard: Enter a Ship-master, and a Botefwaine.

Mafter.

BOte-fwaine.

Botef. Heere Mafter : What cheere ?

Maft. Good : Speake to th'Mariners : fall too't, yarely , or we run our felues a ground, beftirre, beftirre. *Exit.*

Enter Mariners.

Botef. Heigh my hearts, cheerely, cheerely my harts : yare, yare : Take in the toppe-fale : Tend to th'Mafters whiftle : Blow till thou burft thy winde , if roome enough.

Enter Alonfo, Sebaftian, Anthonio, Ferdinando, Gonzalo, and others.

Alon. Good Botefwaine haue care : where's the Mafter ? Play the men.

Botef. I pray now keepe below.

Anth. Where is the Mafter, Bofon ?

Botef. Do you not heare him ? you marre our labour, Keepe your Cabines : you do afsift the ftorme.

Gonz. Nay, good be patient.

Botef. When the Sea is : hence, what cares thefe roarers for the name of King ? to Cabine ; filence : trouble vs not.

Gon. Good, yet remember whom thou haft aboord.

Botef. None that I more loue then my felfe. You are a Counfellor, if you can command thefe Elements to filence, and worke the peace of the prefent, wee will not hand a rope more, vfe your authoritie : If you cannot, giue thankes you haue liu'd fo long , and make your felfe readie in your Cabine for the mifchance of the houre, if it fo hap. Cheerely good hearts : out of our way I fay. *Exit.*

Gon. I haue great comfort from this fellow : methinks he hath no drowning marke vpon him, his complexion is perfect Gallowes : ftand faft good Fate to his hanging, make the rope of his deftiny our cable, for our owne doth little aduantage : If he be not borne to bee hang'd, our cafe is miferable. *Exit.*

Enter Botefwaine.

Botef. Downe with the top-Maft : yare, lower, lower, bring her to Try with Maine-courfe. A plague——

A cry within. *Enter Sebaftian, Anthonio & Gonzalo.*

vpon this howling : they are lowder then the weather, or our office : yet againe ? What do you heere? Shal we giue ore and drowne, haue you a minde to finke ?

Sebaf. A poxe o'your throat, you bawling, blafphemous incharitable Dog.

Botef. Worke you then.

Anth. Hang cur, hang, you whorefon infolent Noyfemaker, we are leffe afraid to be drownde, then thou art.

Gonz. I'le warrant him for drowning , though the Ship were no ftronger then a Nutt-fhell, and as leaky as an vnftanched wench.

Botef. Lay her a hold, a hold , fet her two courfes off to Sea againe, lay her off.

Enter Mariners wet.

Mari. All loft, to prayers, to prayers, all loft.

Botef. What muft our mouths be cold ?

Gonz. The King, and Prince, at prayers, let's affift them, for our cafe is as theirs.

Sebaf. I'am out of patience.

An. We are meerly cheated of our liues by drunkards, This wide-chopt-rafcall, would thou mightft lye drowning the wafhing of ten Tides.

Gonz. Hee'l be hang'd yet, Though euery drop of water fweare againft it, And gape at widft to glut him. *A confufed noyfe within.* Mercy on vs. We fplit, we fplit , Farewell my wife, and children, Farewell brother : we fplit, we fplit, we fplit.

Anth. Let's all finke with' King

Seb. Let's take leaue of him. *Exit.*

Gonz. Now would I giue a thoufand furlongs of Sea, for an Acre of barren ground : Long heath, Browne firrs , any thing ; the wills aboue be done, but I would faine dye a dry death. *Exit.*

Scena Secunda.

Enter Profpero and Miranda.

Mira. If by your Art (my deereft father) you haue Put the wild waters in this Rore, alay them : The skye it feemes would powre down ftinking pitch, But that the Sea, mounting to th' welkins cheeke, Dafhes the fire out. Oh ! I haue fuffered With thofe that I faw fuffer : A braue veffell

A   (Who

Make no Collection of it. Let him shew
His skill in the construction.

 Luc. Philarmonus.

 Sooth. Heere, my good Lord.

 Luc. Read, and declare the meaning.

   Reades.

WHen as a Lyons whelpe, shall to himselfe vnknown, without seeking finde, and bee embrac'd by a peece of tender
Ayre: And when from a stately Cedar shall be lopt, branches,
which being dead many yeares, shall after reuiue, bee ioynted to
the old Stocke, and freshly grow, then shall Posthumus end his
miseries, Britaine be fortunate, and flourish in Peace and Plen-
tie.

Thou *Leonatus* art the Lyons Whelpe,
The fit and apt Construction of thy name
Being *Leonatus*, doth import so much:
The peece of tender Ayre, thy vertuous Daughter,
Which we call *Mollis Aer*, and *Mollis Aer*
We terme it *Mulier*; which *Mulier* I diuine
Is this most constant Wife, who euen now
Answering the Letter of the Oracle,
Vnknowne to you vnsought, were clipt about
With this most tender Aire.

 Cym. This hath some seeming.

 Sooth. The lofty Cedar, Royall *Cymbeline*
Personates thee: And thy lopt Branches, point
Thy two Sonnes forth: who by *Belarius* stolne
For many yeares thought dead, are now reuiu'd
To the Maiesticke Cedar ioyn'd; whose Issue

Promises Britaine, Peace and Plenty.

 Cym. Well,
My Peace we will begin: And *Caius Lucius*,
Although the Victor, we submit to *Cæsar*,
And to the Romane Empire; promising
To pay our wonted Tribute, from the which
We were disswaded by our wicked Queene,
Whom heauens in Iustice both on her, and hers,
Haue laid most heauy hand.

 Sooth. The fingers of the Powres aboue, do tune
The harmony of this Peace: the Vision
Which I made knowne to *Lucius* ere the stroke
Of yet this scarse-cold-Battaile, at this instant
Is full accomplish'd. For the Romane Eagle
From South to West, on wing soaring aloft
Lessen'd her selfe, and in the Beames o'th' Sun
So vanish'd; which fore-shew'd our Princely Eagle
Th'Imperiall *Cæsar*, should againe vnite
His Fauour, with the Radiant *Cymbeline*,
Which shines heere in the West.

 Cym. Laud we the Gods,
And let our crooked Smoakes climbe to their Nostrils
From our blest Altars. Publish we this Peace
To all our Subiects. Set we forward: Let
A Roman, and a Brittish Ensigne waue
Friendly together: so through *Luds-Towne* march,
And in the Temple of great Iupiter
Our Peace wee'l ratifie: Seale it with Feasts.
Set on there: Neuer was a Warre did cease
(Ere bloodie hands were wash'd) with such a Peace.

           Exeunt.

FINIS.

*Printed at the Charges of W. Jaggard, Ed. Blount, I. Smithweeke,
and W. Aspley,* 1623.

126

Sweet Swan of Auon! *what a sight it were*
　　To see thee in our waters yet appeare,
And make those flights vpon the bankes of Thames,
　　That so did take Eliza, *and our* Iames !
But stay, I see thee in the Hemisphere
　　Aduanc'd, and made a Constellation *there !*
Shine forth, thou Starre of Poets, *and with rage,*
　　Or influence, chide, or cheere the drooping Stage;
Which, since thy flight frō hence, hath mourn'd like night,
　　And despaires day, but for thy Volumes *light.*

B **E** N: I O N S O N.

The Family of Shakespeare

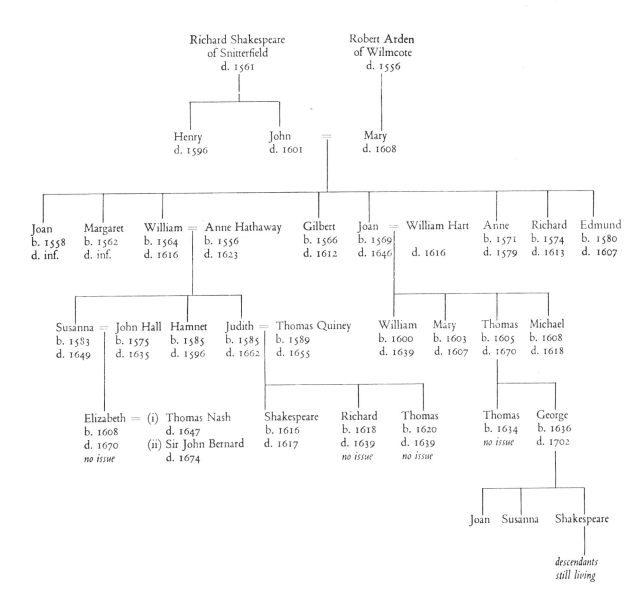

Richard Shakespeare
of Snitterfield
d. 1561

Robert **Arden**
of Wilmcote
d. 1556

Henry
d. 1596

John
d. 1601 = Mary
d. 1608

Joan
b. 1558
d. inf.

Margaret
b. 1562
d. inf.

William = Anne Hathaway
b. 1564 | b. 1556
d. 1616 | d. 1623

Gilbert
b. 1566
d. 1612

Joan = William Hart
b. 1569|
d. 1646| d. 1616

Anne
b. 1571
d. 1579

Richard
b. 1574
d. 1613

Edmund
b. 1580
d. 1607

Susanna = John Hall
b. 1583 | b. 1575
d. 1649 | d. 1635

Hamnet
b. 1585
d. 1596

Judith = Thomas Quiney
b. 1585 | b. 1589
d. 1662 | d. 1655

William
b. 1600
d. 1639

Mary
b. 1603
d. 1607

Thomas
b. 1605
d. 1670

Michael
b. 1608
d. 1618

Elizabeth = (i) Thomas Nash
b. 1608 | d. 1647
d. 1670 | (ii) Sir John Bernard
no issue | d. 1674

Shakespeare
b. 1616
d. 1617

Richard
b. 1618
d. 1639
no issue

Thomas
b. 1620
d. 1639
no issue

Thomas
b. 1634
no issue

George
b. 1636
d. 1702

Joan   Susanna   Shakespeare

*descendants
still living*

ACKNOWLEDGEMENTS

I acknowledge with gratitude the courtesy of those who have given permission
for the reproduction of material in their possession, and I take this opportunity
of thanking Mr Levi Fox, Director of Shakespeare's Birthplace, Mr John
Summerson, Curator of the Sir John Soane Museum, and Mr Arthur Boyars
for their help in obtaining some of the illustrations.

F.E.H.

Frontispiece. This leaden statue of Shakespeare on the wall of the Town Hall at Stratford was presented to the Corporation in 1769 by David Garrick, who organised the Jubilee of that year. It is the work of John Cheere, brother of Sir Henry Cheere, a pupil of Scheemakers. *Photograph by Edwin Smith.*

Page

7 WARWICK FROM BUDBROOKE. *Photograph by Edwin Smith.*

8-9 WARWICKSHIRE IN 1610. Drawn by John Speed for his *Theatre of the Empire of Great Britain*, and engraved by Jodocus Hondius. *British Museum.*

10 SNITTERFIELD CHURCH. Presumably John Shakespeare was christened here, though the register begins only in 1561. *Photograph by Edwin Smith.*

11 ROBERT ARDEN'S HOUSE, WILMCOTE. A typical early 16th century building, with timber frame on a stone foundation. Bought by the Trustees of Shakespeare's Birthplace in 1930. *Photograph by Edwin Smith.*

12 ASTON CANTLOW CHURCH. There is no record of the marriage of John Shakespeare and Mary Arden, as the register begins after that date. *Photograph by Edwin Smith.*

13 SHAKESPEARE'S BIRTHPLACE in 1769, the year of the Garrick Jubilee. The houses are built about a central chimney stack on a stone foundation, the oak frame tied by rafters, the panels filled with wattle and daub. The first known illustration: a drawing by Richard Greene in *The Gentleman's Magazine.*

THE BIRTHPLACE IN 1847. A modern print from a negative taken at the time of its sale to the Birthplace Committee for £3,000. The living-room had been converted into a

butcher's shop (see p. 108). *Trustees of Shakespeare's Birthplace.*

THE BIRTHPLACE IN 1857. Restoration in progress. *Trustees of Shakespeare's Birthplace.*

THE BIRTHPLACE TO-DAY. In 1891 an Act of Parliament incorporated the Trustees and Guardians of Shakespeare's Birthplace, responsible for maintaining property associated with Shakespeare. *Photograph by Edwin Smith.*

14 ENTRY OF SHAKESPEARE'S BAPTISM in the register of Holy Trinity Church, Stratford. In 1600 entries from 1558 onwards were transcribed into this register, each page being signed by the vicar, Richard Byfield, and the churchwardens. *Trustees of Shakespeare's Birthplace.*

ELIZABETH I in 1569, apparently her first portrait as Queen. The painting, by Hans Eworth, forms part of an allegorical group, a kind of Judgment of Paris, in which Elizabeth awards the apple to herself instead of to one of the three goddesses. *From the painting at Hampton Court, by gracious permission of H.M. the Queen.*

15 WILLIAM CECIL, by an unknown artist. Cecil was born in 1520, created Lord Burghley in 1571, Lord Treasurer in 1572, and died in 1598. *National Portrait Gallery*

16 ROBERT DUDLEY, by an unknown artist. Born in 1532, created Earl of Leicester in 1564, he died in 1588. He was the uncle of Philip Sidney and stepfather of the Earl of Essex. *By permission of the Trustees of the Wallace Collection.*

17 CHARLECOTE HOUSE, rebuilt *c.* 1558. Elizabeth knighted Thomas Lucy when she

stayed here in 1566. *Photograph by Edwin Smith.*

18 STRATFORD-UPON-AVON. This aerial view shows all the principal places associated with Shakespeare. *Aerofilms Ltd.*

19 CHURCH OF THE HOLY TRINITY, STRATFORD. The original building is early 13th century, the aisles were added in 1330, the chancel *c.* 1480, and the spire in the 18th century. *Photograph by Edwin Smith.*

20 THE GILDHALL AND SCHOOLROOM. The upper chamber of the Gildhall was converted into the schoolroom of the grammar school in 1564, in place of the old schoolhouse in the quad. Beyond the Gild Chapel is the site of New Place, and beyond that again the house of Thomas Nash, first husband of Shakespeare's granddaughter, Elizabeth Hall. *Photograph by Edwin Smith.*

21 THE GILD CHAPEL, rebuilt by Sir Hugh Clopton, *c.* 1490. There are medieval wall paintings inside. *Photograph by Edwin Smith.*

22 CLOPTON BRIDGE OVER THE AVON. Dr Caroline Spurgeon made the ingenious suggestion that the eddy under the last arch on the far side of the river inspired the description of Collatine's grief in *The Rape of Lucrece:*

As through an arch the violent roaring tide
Outruns the eye that doth behold his haste,
Yet in the eddy boundeth in his pride
Back to the strait that forced him on so fast,
In rage sent out, recall'd in rage, being past:
Even so his sighs, his sorrows, make a saw,
To push grief on and back the same grief draw.
Photograph by Edwin Smith.

23 THE COTSWOLD ESCARPMENT. Meon Hill, near Wincot, four miles south of Stratford. 'Marian Hacket, the fat ale-wife' of *The Taming of the Shrew,* lived at Wincot: In 1591

'Sara Hacket, the daughter of Robert Hacket' was baptised at Quinton, within the parish of which Wincot lies. *Photograph by Edwin Smith.*

24 STRATFORD GRAMMAR SCHOOL. The schoolroom was originally the over-hall of the Gild of the Holy Cross. *Photograph by Edwin Smith.*

25 THE GENEVAN BIBLE, 1560. Prepared in Geneva by refugee reformers during the Marian persecution, it is sometimes known as the 'Breeches Bible', from its rendering of *Genesis* iii. 7: 'They sewed fig tree leaves together and made themselves breeches'. *British Museum.*

LILY'S LATIN GRAMMAR, 1567, the First (English) Part. William Lily was the first High Master of St Paul's School, and grandfather of the dramatist John Lyly. *Folger Shakespeare Library, Washington.*

26 SIR FRANCIS DRAKE (*c.* 1540-96), aged 43. *British Museum.*

27 PERRAN ROUND. Only two medieval theatres remain, both in Cornwall. The interior of Perran Round is 130 feet across, the banks about 12 feet high. A tunnel, or 'conveyor', ran under the stage, ending in a pit near the middle of the arena. This reconstruction, by the author, is based mainly on stage directions in the Cornish miracle plays.

28-29 LONDON FROM THE NORTH, *c.* 1600. An engraving, apparently unique, inserted in the manuscript journal of Abram Booth, an agent of the Dutch East India Company. *Library of the University of Utrecht.*

29 THE CURTAIN THEATRE, built by Henry Laneman, 1576-7. Detail from the left of the *View of London.* The neighbouring Theatre had been removed, and this is the only known view of one of the two first London playhouses.

29 *Gorboduc*, 1565: the first edition, surreptitiously printed. It is the first English tragedy to be written in the classical Senecan manner. *Huntington Library, San Marino, California.*

30 BLACKFRIARS FROM BANKSIDE. The boys' theatre was in one of the buildings behind Blackfriars Stairs (see p. 111). From J. C. Visscher's View of London, dated 1616. Visscher, who may never have been in London, based his panorama on Norden's *View* in *Civitas Londini* (p. 40-41). *British Museum.*

31 THE QUEEN'S INTERLUDERS AT STRATFORD. The payment is the third entry. From the Stratford Council Book, 1568-9. *Trustees of Shakespeare's Birthplace.*

'THE HONORABLE ENTERTAINEMENT gieuen to the Queenes Maiestie in Progresse, at Elvetham,' 1591. Shakespeare probably had this woodcut from this pamphlet in mind when in *A Midsummer Night's Dream*, II. i he makes Oberon describe a water pageant with fireworks, and Elizabeth as 'a fair vestal throned by the west'. The Elvetham Entertainment must have resembled the one at Kenilworth. *British Museum.*

32 THE GOLDEN HIND. In April, 1581, Elizabeth knighted Drake on board when it anchored at Deptford. There it was preserved for a century before being broken up. From the map of Drake's voyage, by Jodocus Hondius. *British Museum.*

33 *Euphues*, 1579: the first edition. Shakespeare parodied rather than imitated euphuism, the artificial speech of the period; for example, Falstaff in 1 *Henry IV*: 'Though the camomile, the more it is trodden on the faster it grows, yet youth, the more it is wasted the sooner it wears.' *British Museum.*

PLUTARCH'S *Lives*, translated by Sir Thomas North: the first edition, 1579. Richard Field, the Stratford boy, was apprenticed to Vautrollier, the finest printer of his age (see p. 53). *British Museum.*

34 TEMPLE GRAFTON CHURCH, a drawing by James Saunders *c*. 1800. It was rebuilt in the 19th century, and unfortunately the register does not begin until 1695. *Trustees of Shakespeare's Birthplace.*

SHAKESPEARE'S MARRIAGE BOND. The first four lines, in Latin, are the bond proper, in which Sandells and Richardson bind themselves in a surety of £40 on behalf of Shakespeare. The remainder is in English: 'The condicion of this obligacion ys suche that if herafter there shall not appere any Lawfull Lett or impediment . . . but that William Shagspere . . . and Anne Hathwey of Stratford . . . maiden may lawfully solennize matrimony together . . . then the said obligacion to be voyd . . .' *Diocesan Registry, Worcester.*

35 THE HATHAWAY FARMHOUSE at Shottery, originally called Hewland. In the 18th century it was converted into three cottages, acquired by the Birthplace Trustees in 1892. *Photograph by Edwin Smith.*

SHAKESPEARE'S MARRIAGE LICENCE. The clerk's erroneous entry in the Bishop of Worcester's Register: 'Item eodem die similis emanavit licencia inter Wm Shaxpere et Annam Whateley de Temple Grafton.' 'Item, on the same day [27 Nov. 1582] a similar licence was issued between W.S. and A.W. of T.G.' *Diocesan Registry, Worcester.*

36 THE BAPTISM OF SHAKESPEARE'S CHILDREN. The entries in the register of Holy Trinity Church. *Trustees of Shakespeare's Birthplace.*

37 HAMPTON LUCY FROM CHARLECOTE PARK. 'Lettyce the Daughter', and 'Jeames the sonne of Henrye Shakespere' were christened

in Hampton Lucy church in 1582 and 1585 respectively. James was buried there in Sept. 1589. This Henry Shakespeare was probably the poet's uncle. *Photograph by Edwin Smith.*

38 WESTMINSTER, from John Norden's *Speculum Britanniae*, 1593. *British Museum.*

39 WHITEHALL, from J. C. Visscher's *View of London* (see p. 30 note). *British Museum.*

40-41 VIEW OF LONDON, 1600, from *Civitas Londini*, drawn by John Norden. This is the source of Visscher's *View* (see p. 30). The Swan and Beargarden are clearly visible. Almost hidden in the trees to the south-east of the Beargarden are the Rose and Globe. All are shown as polygonal, possibly an error or an 'artistic' touch by the unknown engraver. *Royal Library, Stockholm.*

42 MARY, QUEEN OF SCOTS in 1578, aged 36. A portrait attributed to P. Oudry. *National Portrait Gallery.*

43 *Campaspe*, 1584: the first edition. John Lyly (c. 1554-1606) was the author of *Euphues* (p. 33). *British Museum.*

Tamburlaine, 1590: the first edition. Though there is little direct evidence that Marlowe wrote the play there is no doubt that it is his. *Bodleian Library, Oxford.*

44-45 THE SPANISH ARMADA. The medallions show the commanders of the English ships. By Hendrick Cornelius Vroom (1566-1619), from *The Tapestry Hangings in the House of Lords*, by John Pine, 1739. *British Museum.*

47 ROBERT DEVEREUX, 2nd EARL OF ESSEX (1567-1601). Painted in 1597 by an unknown artist. *National Portrait Gallery.*

SIR WALTER RALEIGH (c. 1552-1618). Painted in Armada year by an unknown

artist. For thirteen years before his execution he was imprisoned by James I. *National Portrait Gallery.*

QUEEN ELIZABETH, aged 59. Painted by an unknown artist to commemorate her visit in 1592 to Ditchley, Oxfordshire, on which county she is standing. *National Portrait Gallery.*

48 SIR PHILIP SIDNEY. He was only thirty-two when mortally wounded in the Netherlands at the beginning of the war with Spain, 1586. The quotation is from the elegy of his friend, Fulke Greville. *National Portrait Gallery: artist unknown.*

The Faerie Queene. St George and the Dragon, from the first edition of Books I-III, 1590. *British Museum.*

49 *The Spanish Tragedy*, the first extant edition, 1592(?). Kyd was probably the author of the original lost play of *Hamlet*, Shakespeare's version of which is the most famous of all tragedies of revenge. *British Museum.*

Greenes Groatsworth of Wit, 1592. 'Sweete boy' is Nashe; 'thou no less deserving' probably Peele. Marlowe is addressed as 'the famous gracer of Tragedians . . . who hath said . . . There is no God'. *British Museum.*

50 HENSLOWE'S *Diary* is really an account book in which he entered his receipts. The entries are headed, 'In the name of god Amen 1591 begininge the 19 of Febreary my lord Stranges mene as ffoloweth 1591'. The new year then began on March 25th, so that February 1591 is 1592 according to our reckoning. The first entry is Greene's *Friar Bacon*, 17s. 3d.; the third Greene's *Orlando Furioso*, 16s. 6d.; the seventh Marlowe's *Jew of Malta*, 50s. Shakespeare's 1 *Henry VI* is the twelfth, its receipts £3 16s. 8d., the highest of the season, its popularity so great that it was given fifteen times. Henslowe died a few

weeks before Shakespeare. *Dulwich College, by permission of the Governors.*

50 *Pierce Penilesse*, 1592: the first edition. Nashe is defending plays, and the Talbot reference is almost certainly to Shakespeare's 1 *Henry VI*. *British Museum.*

51 *Kind-Harts Dreame: Conteining fiue Apparitions, with their Inuectiues against abuses raigning*, 1592: the first edition. One of the apparitions is Greene, 'of face amible, of body well proportioned'. *British Museum.*

53 *Venus and Adonis*, the first quarto. Field had now taken over the Vautrollier press and used the same device (see p. 33). The quotation is from Ovid's *Amores* I. xv., rendered by Marlowe:

Let base-conceited wits admire vile things:
Fair Phoebus lead me to the Muses' springs.

British Museum.

54 *The Rape of Lucrece*. The only quarto, all other editions being in octavo. *Bodleian Library, Oxford.*

HENRY WRIOTHESLEY, 3rd EARL OF SOUTH-AMPTON (1573-1630). A painting in the possession of the Duke of Portland at Welbeck Abbey.

55 WILLIAM HERBERT, 3rd EARL OF PEM-BROKE (1580-1630). The Folio of 1623 was dedicated to him and his brother, the Earl of Montgomery. A painting by Van Dyck in the possession of Lord Herbert at Wilton House.

Shakespeare's Sonnets, 1609, the only early edition. Thorpe became a member of the Stationers' Company in 1594 and was active for thirty years. *British Museum.*

56 *Willobie His Avisa*, 1594. Henry Willoughby was related by marriage to Thomas Russell,

one of the overseers of Shakespeare's will. *British Museum.*

57 *The First Part of the Contention*, the 'bad' quarto of 2 *Henry VI*, so bad that until recently it was thought to be the source-play used by Shakespeare. *Bodleian Library, Oxford.*

58 *Titus Andronicus*, a drawing probably made by Henry Peacham in 1594. It illustrates, not quite accurately, the first scene: 'Tamora pleadinge for her sonnes going to execution'. Aaron the Moor, and presumably therefore, Othello, is conceived as a negro, and there is some attempt at historical costume for the chief characters. From the *Harley Papers* in the possession of the Marquis of Bath at Longleat.

59 WILLIAM KEMPE, from the title page of his *Nine Days' Wonder*, 1600, an account of his dance from London to Norwich in 1599. He died a few years later. *Bodleian Library, Oxford.*

HENRY CAREY, 1st LORD HUNSDON (c. 1524-96). Lord Chamberlain, and the nephew of Anne Boleyn. *British Museum.*

RICHARD BURBAGE (c. 1568-1619), played 'young Hamlett, ould Heironymoe, Kind Leer, the greued Moore, and more beside'. He and Alleyn were the greatest actors of the age. *Dulwich College, by permission of the Governors.*

60 EDWARD ALLEYN (1566-1626). He retired in 1604, having made a fortune. His first wife was Henslowe's stepdaughter, his second the daughter of John Donne. He founded Dulwich College, where this portrait is preserved. *By permission of the Governors.*

61 GEORGE CHAPMAN (c. 1559-1634). Shakespeare's sonnet 86, 'Was it the proud full sail of his great verse', may refer to Chapman. He is chiefly remembered for his translation of Homer, which inspired Keats. *British Museum.*

61 MICHAEL DRAYTON (1563–1631). The girl he loved married Sir Henry Rainsford of Clifford Chambers, near Stratford, where he used to stay. *National Portrait Gallery: artist unknown.*

62 BENJAMIN JONSON (1572–1637). He complained that 'Shakespeare wanted art', meaning that he did not follow the classical 'rules', yet he wrote the splendid elegy in the Folio, 'To the memory of my beloved, Mr William Shakespeare'. Apparently the portrait is a copy of one at Knole by Gerard Honthorst. *National Portrait Gallery.*

63 *Sir Thomas More.* The last of the three pages, lines 96–147, thought by some to be in Shakespeare's handwriting. The passage begins,

all   marry god forbid that

moo   nay certainly yo^u ar
    for to the king god hath his offyc lent
    of dread of Iustyce, power and
      Comaund
    hath bid him rule, and willd yo^u to
      obay

The manuscript, *Harley 7368*, is in the British Museum.

65 SHAKESPEARE AS PAYEE. 'To Willm Kempe Willm Shakespeare & Richarde Burbage seruantes to the Lord Chambleyne vpon the councelles warr^t dated at Whitehall xv^{to} Martii 1594 for twoe seuerall comedies or Enterludes shewed by them before her Matie in xrmas tyme laste paste viz^d vpon St Stephens daye & Innocentes daye xiii^l vj^s viij^d and by waye of her ma^{tes} Rewarde vj^l xiij^s iiij^d.' From the accounts of the Treasurer of the Chamber. *Public Record Office.*

GREENWICH PALACE, originally called Pleasaunce or Placentia. Here Henry VII died, and Henry VIII, Mary and Elizabeth were born. Demolished by Charles II,

Greenwich Hospital was built on its site by Wren. A drawing by Anthony van Wyndgaerde. *Ashmolean Museum, Oxford.*

66 THE HALL OF GRAY'S INN, built 1556–60, and gutted during an air raid in 1941. *Copyright Raphael Tuck & Sons Ltd.*

67 THE SWAN THEATRE. The sketch was discovered by the German scholar, K. T. Gaedertz in 1888, from which date modern research may be said to begin. De Witt added a note that the Swan was built of a concrete of flints, with wooden columns painted to resemble marble, and that it would seat 3,000.

68 ENTRY OF HAMNET'S DEATH, in the register of Holy Trinity Church, Stratford. *Trustees of Shakespeare's Birthplace.*

69 HARVARD HOUSE. The date, 1596, can be seen on the centre boss beneath the middle window. John Harvard (1607–38) went to America and bequeathed money and books to the College that became Harvard University. *Photograph by Edwin Smith.*

70 THE GRANT OF ARMS. Line 13 reads that 'John Shakespeare of Stratford vppon Avon in the counte of Warwick whose parentes and late antecessors were for their valiant and faithful services advanced and rewarded by the most prudent prince King Henry the seventh . . .' It may be so, though there is no record of such services, and the citation may have been a fiction to justify the grant, which was in fact challenged in 1602 by Ralph Broke, York Herald. *A photograph supplied by the Shakespeare Birthplace Trust of the draft in the College of Arms.*

71 GEORGE CAREY, 2nd LORD HUNSDON (1547–1603). A miniature, in the possession of the Duke of Buccleuch, by the great Elizabethan 'limner' Nicholas Hilliard. It has recently been questioned whether this really

is a portrait of Lord Hunsdon. *From a print in the Victoria and Albert Museum.*

71 WILLIAM WAYTE'S PETITION, Nov. 1596, from the rolls of the Court of Queen's Bench, discovered by Dr Leslie Hotson in 1930. The abbreviated Latin, expanded, reads:

Anglia. *scire scilicet* Will*el*m*us* Wayte pet*it securitates* pacis *versus* Will*el*m*um* Shakspere, Franciscu*m* Langley, Dorotheam Soer uxor*em* Joha*nn*is Soer & Annam Lee, ob metu*m* mortis &c.

England. Be it known that W.W. craves sureties of the peace against W.S., F.L., D.S., wife of John Soer, & A.L. for fear of death &c. *Public Record Office.*

72 SIR THOMAS LUCY (1532–1600), the effigy in Charlecote church. His wife, Joyce, 'in love to her husband most faithful and true', died in 1596. *Photograph by Edwin Smith.*

73 NEW PLACE. The original 'grete house', built by Sir Hugh Clopton and bought by Shakespeare, was pulled down about 1702. This drawing, the only known authentic illustration, was made by George Vertue 'by memory' in 1737, and represents the Church Street front, 'a long gallery &c and for servants', the 'real dwelling house' being behind. *British Museum.*

75 THE SITE OF NEW PLACE. The second New Place, 'a handsome brick house', was pulled down in 1759 by its irate owner, Rev. Francis Gastrell, because he thought the rates too high. To-day only the foundations remain. *Photograph by Edwin Smith.*

77 *Love's Labour's Lost,* the first quarto. *British Museum.*

78 *Palladis Tamia: Wits Treasury,* 1598, is the second of a short series of books called *Wit's Commonwealth,* by various authors. Francis Meres (1565–1647) was a graduate of both

Cambridge and Oxford. In 1602 he became rector and schoolmaster at Wing, Rutland. *British Museum.*

79 *Every Man in his Humour,* cast of the first performance, from the Folio edition of Jonson's *Works,* 1616. *British Museum.*

80 RICHARD QUINEY'S LETTER. It begins, 'Loveinge Contreyman, I am bolde of yowe as of a ffrende, craveinge yowre helpe with xxx^{ll} vppon Mr Bushells & my securytee or Mr Myttons with me. Mr Rosswell is nott come to London as yeate & I have especiall cawse. Yowe shall ffrende me muche in helpeinge me out of all the debettes I owe in London, I thancke god, & muche quiet my mynde which wolde nott be indebted. I am nowe towardes the Cowrte . . .'

Richard was on his way to see the Privy Council in a successful attempt to get taxation relief for Stratford, badly hit by the fires. He died in 1602, during his second term as bailiff. *Trustees of Shakespeare's Birthplace.*

81 BANKSIDE, 1600, from *Civitas Londini,* by John Norden. The Rose is miscalled 'The Star', a name otherwise unknown. All the theatres are shown as cylindrical, the most authoritative indication of their shape. *Royal Library, Stockholm.*

82 BANKSIDE, from Visscher's *View* (see note to p. 30). Visscher, copying Norden's *View* (p. 40) failed to see the Globe and gave its name to the Rose. The theatres are shown as polygonal. *British Museum.*

83 THE GLOBE THEATRE. There may have been rails round the apron stage when it was built, though the first real evidence is in Middleton's *Black Book,* 1604: 'the stage-rails of this earthen globe'. *A reconstruction by the author.*

84 THE STATIONERS' REGISTER, 1600. '23 Augusti. Andrew Wyse William Aspley. Entred for their copies vnder the handes of

the wardens Two bookes, the one called Muche a Doo about nothinge. Thother the second parte of the history of Kinge Henry the iiijth with the humours of Sir John Falstaff: Wrytten by master Shakespere. xijd.' *Stationers' Hall, by permission of the Worshipful Company of Stationers.*

84 *Rosalynde: Euphues Golden Legacie,* 1590, written by Thomas Lodge on his voyage to the Azores. *British Museum.*

85 'IT, WAS A LOVER AND HIS LASS.' Morley was one of the greatest of Elizabethan composers, particularly of lute songs and madrigals. He died, aged 46, in 1603. He was probably a friend of Shakespeare's. His setting of the song comes from a unique copy of his *First Booke of Ayres,* 1600, in the Folger Shakespeare Library, Washington.

86 *Poetaster or The Arraignment:* the first quarto, 1602. *British Museum.*

87 *The Returne from Pernassus: or the Scourge of Simony.* 'Publiquely acted by the Students in Saint Iohns Colledge in Cambridge.' The first quarto, 1606. *British Museum.*

The Tragicall Historie of Hamlet Prince of Denmarke. 'By William Shakespeare. As it hath beene diuerse times acted by his Highnesse seruants in the Cittie of London: as also in the two Vniuersities of Cambridge and Oxford, and else-where.' The 'bad' quarto, 1603; how bad may be seen by comparing this passage with the full text in II.ii. *Bodleian Library, Oxford.*

88 SHAKESPEARE'S ESTATE of 127 acres at Old Stratford. *Photograph by Edwin Smith.*

THE CONVEYANCE of the Old Stratford estate, 1 May 1602. 'This indenture . . . Betweene William Combe of Warrwicke . . . Esquier, and John Combe of Olde Stretford . . . gentleman, on the one partie,

And William Shakespere of Stretford vppon Avon . . . gentleman, on thother partye, Witnesseth that . . . in consideracion of the somme of three hundred and twentie poundes . . .' It was 'Sealed and deliuered to Gilbert Shakespere, to the vse of the within named William Shakespere'. *Trustees of Shakespeare's Birthplace.*

89 RICHMOND PALACE, the medieval Sheen. Rebuilt by Henry VII, James I gave it to Prince Henry, after whose death it fell into decay. There are morris dancers in the foreground. A painting of about 1620 by an unknown artist. *By permission of the Syndics of the Fitzwilliam Museum, Cambridge.*

90 JAMES I and VI, 1610. Probably by John de Critz. *By permission of the Trustees of the National Maritime Museum, Greenwich.*

91 THE SPECIAL COMMISSION appointing 'William Shackespeare and others' the King's Servants, 19 May 1603. 'James by the grace of god . . . Knowe yee that Wee . . . haue licenced . . . theise our Servauntes Lawrence Fletcher, William Shakespeare, Richard Burbage, Augustyne Phillippes, Iohn Heninges, Henrie Condell, William Sly, Robert Armyn, Richard Cowly, and the rest of theire Assosiates to vse and exercise the Arte and faculty of playinge Comedies, Tragedies, histories, Enterludes . . . aswell for the recreation of our lovinge Subjectes, as for our Solace and pleasure.' Fletcher came from Scotland with James, and was merely an honorary member of the company. *Public Record Office.*

92 MIDDLE TEMPLE HALL. 'At our feast wee had a play called Twelue Night or What You Will, much like the Commedy of Errores.' From the *Diary* of John Manningham. *Picture Post Library.*

THE FIRST SHAKESPEARE ANECDOTE, 13 March 1602. 'Vpon a tyme when Burbidge played Rich. 3. there was a citizen greue soe farr in liking with him that before shee went from the play shee appointed him to come that night vnto hir by the name of Ri: the 3. Shakespeare overhearing their conclusion went before, was intertained, and at his game ere Burbidge came. Then message being brought that Rich. the 3.ᵈ was at the dore, Shakespeare caused returne to be made that William the Conquerour was before Rich. the 3. Shakespeare's name William. *(Mr Curle)*.' From the *Diary* of John Manningham. His informant, Edward Curle, was a fellow student at the Middle Temple. *British Museum.*

93 WILTON HOUSE. The central part is all that remains of the original Tudor house, rebuilt by Inigo Jones after the fire of about 1647. Lady Pembroke is said to have written to her son, 'We have the man Shakespeare with us'. *National Building Record.*

94 MOUNTJOY'S HOUSE. From the map of London attributed to Ralph Agas, printed in 1633. *British Museum.*

95 THE SOMERSET HOUSE CONFERENCE, August 1604. The English delegation, on the right, consists of Sir Robert Cecil; the Earl of Northampton; Charles Blount, Earl of Devon, who defeated Tyrone after Essex's failure; the Earl of Nottingham, Lord Admiral at the time of the Armada, and patron of the company of players; Thomas Sackville, Earl of Dorset, part author of *Gorboduc*. The leader of the Spanish delegation is the Constable of Castile, on whom Shakespeare and the King's men attended. The painting is attributed to M. Gheeraerts II. *National Portrait Gallery.*

96 THE REVELS ACCOUNTS for 1604-5, made out by the Master of the Revels, Edmund Tilney, showing expenses incurred for the Court performance of plays. Only two

Accounts of the period of Shakespeare's career have survived. *Public Record Office.*

97 *The Masque of Blackness.* One of the twelve masquers. 'The colours azure and silver, but returned on the top with a scroll and antique dressing of feathers, and jewels interlaced with ropes of pearl. And for the front, ear, neck and wrists, the ornament was of the most choice and orient pearl.' *Devonshire Collection, Chatsworth. By permission of the Trustees of the Chatsworth Settlement.*

98 CLOPTON HOUSE: the old doorway. The rest of the house was rebuilt about 1700. *Photograph by Edwin Smith.*

99 *The Chronicles of England, Scotland and Ireland, 1577:* the first edition. When Raphael Holinshed died, about 1580, he was steward of the manor of Packwood, near Stratford. *British Museum.*

101 *Select Observations,* by John Hall (1575-1635). Unfortunately his notes begin after Shakespeare's death, but he records how he cured his wife and daughter of various ailments. *Trustees of Shakespeare's Birthplace.*

HALL'S CROFT. The house was bought by the Shakespeare Birthplace Trust in 1949. *Photograph by Edwin Smith.*

102 JOHN FLETCHER (1579-1625). Born at Rye, Sussex, he probably went to Cambridge. His father was Bishop of London. *National Portrait Gallery: artist unknown.*

FRANCIS BEAUMONT (1584-1616). The son of Sir Francis Beaumont, he was an Oxford and Inner Temple man. According to John Aubrey, Beaumont and Fletcher 'lived together on the Banke Side, not far from the Playhouse, both batchelors; lay together; had one wench in the house between them, which they did so admire; the same cloathes and cloake, &c., between them'. In the possession of Lord Sackville at Knole. *Artist unknown.*

103 SIMON FORMAN's *Booke of Plaies*. Forman (1552-1611), an Oxford man, practised in London, where he was imprisoned for having no diploma, though eventually he was granted one by Cambridge. He died 12 Sept. 1611 while crossing the Thames in a boat, probably by suicide. His note begins, 'Obserue ther howe Lyontes the kinge of Cicillia was overcom with Jelosy of his wife with the kinge of Bohemia his frind . . .' On the next page he describes Autolycus, 'the Rog that cam in all tottered like coll pixci', and concludes, 'Beware of trustinge feined beggars or fawninge fellouss'. *Bodleian Library, Oxford.*

SHAKESPEARE's *Sonnets*, 1609. See note to p. 55.

104 THE REVELS ACCOUNT for 1611-12 (see p. 96 and note). Tilney died in 1610 and the Master of the Revels was now Sir George Buck. *A King and No King* and *Cupid's Revenge* are by Beaumont and Fletcher. *Tu Quoque* was the popular name for *The City Gallant*, a comedy by Jo. Cooke. *The Silver Age* and *Lucrece* are Heywood's. The authors of the other plays are unknown. *Public Record Office.*

105 SHAKESPEARE'S DEPOSITION AND SIGNA-TURE in the case of *Belott v. Mountjoy*. Shakespeare's evidence, of which this is the conclusion, was written by a clerk. The last two lines, not quite complete in the illustration, read, '[he knoweth not what] implementes and necessaries of houshould stuffe [the defendant gaue the plaintiff] in marriadge with his daughter Marye.' The Belott-Mountjoy Suit was discovered by Prof. C. W. Wallace of the University of Nebraska in 1910. *Public Record Office.*

106 THE MARRIAGE OF PRINCESS ELIZABETH AND FREDERICK V, ELECTOR PALATINE, 14 February 1613. Frederick lost the crown of Bohemia and his Electorate, and died in 1632. Elizabeth, 'Queen of Hearts', died in England in 1662. She was the mother of Rupert of the Rhine, and grandmother of George I. From a German broadsheet, 1613. *British Museum.*

106 QUEEN ANNE (1574-1619). The daughter of Frederick II of Denmark, she married James in 1589 when he was king of Scotland only. A miniature by Isaac Oliver at Windsor Castle. *By gracious permission of H.M. the Queen.*

HENRY, PRINCE OF WALES (1594-1612). Instead of an enlightened Henry IX, England had Charles I and a Civil War. A miniature by Isaac Oliver. *By permission of the Syndics of the Fitzwilliam Museum, Cambridge.*

107 THE BLACKFRIARS GATEHOUSE: THE CONVEYANCE, 10 March 1613. 'William Shakespeare of Stratford Vpon Avon' pays Henry Walker £140 for a tenement 'part of which is erected over a great gate'. The famous Mermaid meetings took place on the first Friday of the month, and it was just at this time that Johnson was charged with serving meat instead of fish on Fridays in Lent. *Guildhall Library, London.*

THE BLACKFRIARS GATEHOUSE: THE MORTGAGE to Walker for £60, apparently as security against payment of the balance, 11 March 1613. Shakespeare leased the house to one John Robinson. It was destroyed by the Great Fire of 1666. *British Museum.*

108 THE SWAN AND MAIDENHEAD. About 1808 the eastern part of the Birthplace property was fronted with red brick (see p. 13). A lithograph by C. Graf, 1851. *Trustees of Shakespeare's Birthplace.*

109 JOHN COMBE. The verses that Shakespeare is said to have 'fanned up' are,

Ten in the hundred must lie in his graue,
But a hundred to ten whether God will him haue.

Who then must be interr'd in this Tombe?
Oh (quoth the Diuell) my John a Combe.

It is only a legend, and the verses are merely a variation on an old theme. *Photograph by Edwin Smith.*

110 THE CROWN TAVERN, OXFORD. Towards the end of his career in London Shakespeare probably made the journey to Stratford two or three times a year; Oxford was a convenient place to break the journey, and he may well have stayed with the Davenants and been godfather of William, born in 1606. On the other hand, he left 20s. to his godson William Walker, and there is no mention of William Davenant in his will. When Davenant was a knight, Poet Laureate and in his cups he used to like to think that Shakespeare was his father.

The Crown Tavern is now 3 Cornmarket Street, where the painted bedroom-walls were discovered in 1927. *Photograph by W. R. Rose, by permission of Mr E. W. Attwood.*

THOMAS GREENE'S NOTE. 'Sept. W Shakspeare's tellyng J Greene that J [I] was not able to beare the encloseinge of Welcombe.' This was inserted between the entry of 14 Aug.—'Mr Barber dyed'—and that of 5 Sept. —'his sending James for the executours of Mr Barber to agree as ys sayd with them for Mr Barbers interest.' Thomas Barber was a landowner, and the 'his' of the last entry is probably William Combe, the leader of the enclosure movement. The note on Shakespeare is not very clear, for Greene was a titheholder and would probably gain by enclosure. A fortnight before Shakespeare's death he was replaced as town clerk by Francis Collins. *Trustees of Shakespeare's Birthplace.*

111 THE SECOND GLOBE. After 1614 the 'Beere bayting house' was also a theatre, the Hope. From the *Long View* of London, 1647, by Wenceslas Hollar. *Guildhall Library, London.*

113 SHAKESPEARE'S WILL: the last page. Probably written by Collins's clerk, it begins, 'Males of the bodies of the said . . .' The 'Item, I gyve vnto my wief my second best bed with the furniture' is the insertion above the ninth line. John and Susanna Hall are residuary legatees and appointed executors, Thomas Russell and Francis Collins overseers. On the left are the witnesses' signatures, on the right the probate endorsement, 22 June 1616. Shakespeare signed each of the three sheets and probably wrote the 'By me'. These three signatures, the two of the Gatehouse transaction and that of the deposition are the only writing that can definitely be claimed as his (see p. 63 and note). *Somerset House, London.*

114 ENTRY OF SHAKESPEARE'S BURIAL in the register of Holy Trinity Church, Stratford. *Trustees of Shakespeare's Birthplace.*

115 THE CHANCEL OF HOLY TRINITY CHURCH. Shakespeare's monument is the first on the left wall, beyond the door, his grave in the sanctuary floor below. John Combe's tomb is to the left of the altar. *Photograph by Edwin Smith.*

117 SHAKESPEARE'S MONUMENT. The monument itself is marble, the bust of painted Cotswold stone. The Latin inscription reads:
In judgment a Nestor, in genius a Socrates, in art a Virgil:
The earth covers him, the people mourn him, Olympus has him.
Photograph by Edwin Smith.

119 THE FIRST FOLIO: TITLE PAGE. The engraving is by Martin Droeshout, son of a Flemish immigrant. He was only fifteen when Shakespeare died, and probably worked from a line drawing by some unknown artist. The engraving exists in two states, the second of which, more heavily worked, is reproduced here. This portrait and the bust, the proportions of which agree,

are the only two authentic likenesses of Shakespeare, though not necessarily very accurate ones. *British Museum.*

121 THE FIRST FOLIO: THE PREFACE. Note that Heminge and Condell claim to have replaced the 'bad' quarto texts by those of the original manuscripts, and that there was scarcely a 'blot' (erasure) in Shakespeare's papers.

122 WILLIAM SLY, died 1608. *Dulwich College, by permission of the Governors.*

JOHN LOWIN (1576-1669?). He became a sharer in 1604, and stayed with the company until the closing of the theatres in 1642, when he turned innkeeper. He played Morose, Volpone, Epicure Mammon and Bosola. *Ashmolean Museum, Oxford.*

NATHAN FIELD (1587-1620). As one of the Chapel Children he was a great favourite of Jonson's. *Dulwich College, by permission of the Governors.*

123 THE FIRST FOLIO: THE ACTOR LIST. These are the sharers in the Chamberlain's-King's company from 1594 to 1623. The list is approximately chronological.

124 THE FIRST FOLIO: THE CATALOGUE OF PLAYS. Only half of them had previously been published, and only fourteen with good texts. By an oversight *Troilus and Cressida,* the first play in the Tragedy section, was omitted from the Catalogue.

125 THE FIRST FOLIO: *The Tempest.* The last of Shakespeare's plays is the first in the Folio, and its stage directions the most detailed. Some plays merely give entries, others are divided only into acts, and six have no division at all.

126 THE FIRST FOLIO: *Cymbeline.* The last page.

127 THE GRAVE OF SHAKESPEARE. On his right lies Thomas Nash, first husband of his granddaughter, Elizabeth Hall, on his left his wife, Anne. *Photograph by Edwin Smith.*

128 JONSON'S ELEGY 'To the memory of my beloued, the Author, Mr. William Shakespeare, and what he hath left vs.' The last ten lines. From the First Folio.

INDEX OF ARTISTS

Page numbers in italics refer to the pictures